TOILET TRAINING
IN LESS THAN A DAY

is clearly and sympathetically written, with explicit drawings to demonstrate every single step in the training procedure. Enjoy, as thousands of parents have, the many rewards you can expect from this wonderful new teaching technique.

But as important as the new method is for parents, the major concern is for the child. Spanking and anger are definitely excluded. During the training the child is hugged, praised, given treats, and made the center of loving attention.

Typically, at the end of training, the child is filled with pride and a sense of accomplishment. This increased happiness of the child is the most gratifying aspect of the Azrin–Foxx technique.

Toilet Training
in Less Than a Day

Nathan H. Azrin, Ph.D.
and Richard M. Foxx, Ph.D.

PUBLISHED BY POCKET BOOKS NEW YORK

POCKET BOOKS, a division of Simon & Schuster Inc
1230 Avenue of the Americas, New York, N Y 10020

Published by arrangement with Simon and Schuster
Library of Congress Catalog Card Number: 73-17618

ISBN: 0-671-43660-0

First Pocket Books printing June, 1976

43 42 41 40 39 38 37 36 35 34

POCKET and colophon are registered trademarks
of Simon & Schuster, Inc

Printed in the U.S.A

ACKNOWLEDGMENTS

Many individuals assisted in the development of the new training procedure. R. C. Steck and P. Levison provided the necessary administrative support and encouragement. Afton Jarvis and Angela Foss served as trainers for many of the children in the formal study. The development of the toilet-training procedure was made possible by the Division of Research Services of the Illinois Department of Mental Health. Preliminary sketches were drawn by Joanna Flores. Tim and Greg Hildebrandt drew the illustrations that appear in this book.

We are especially appreciative of the cooperation and support of the many mothers and children who participated in the toilet-training project during its initial development.

CONTENTS

FOREWORD

The development of the new method of toilet training has been an exciting adventure for us.

The story of how the new procedure came to be developed is best told if we describe first who we are. We are psychologists who study what is involved in learning and how learning can be made more rapid. Like many other psychologists who study the learning process, we felt obligated to apply new discoveries about learning to those persons who suffer the most from the problem—namely, the profoundly retarded persons who have such a deficit in learning ability that they must be confined to an institution. Typically, the profoundly retarded person is so helpless that he cannot dress himself, nor feed himself properly, nor speak, nor toilet himself. He is perhaps the most ignored and least fortunate element in human society.

In our research with the profoundly retarded, our objective was to elevate the level of functioning and happiness of the retarded. The results were gratifying. The profoundly retarded could learn, by the newly developed procedures, to eat as well as normal persons; they could be motivated by special motivational procedures to be enthusiastic and eager; they could learn to refrain from physical aggression; and they could be taught to groom and dress themselves properly. A message was becoming clear: the plight of the profoundly retarded person was not hopeless; he could be taught to function in a more normal manner by intensive training programs.

One of the major unsolved problems for the profoundly retarded was toileting; most of them are incapable of toileting themselves even as adults. Our efforts with toilet training of the retarded yielded results as gratifying as the results for the other activities. We devised a method that was successful in training about 95 percent of them, and in an average time of only three days, to toilet all by themselves. Forty years of pants wetting and soiling could be ended by a few days of intensive training.

The next stage in our research was to develop toilet-training procedures for persons who were only moderately retarded or not retarded and who had ample learning ability. For if the profoundly retarded could be taught in about three days, mildly retarded or normal children should be able to learn even faster. We therefore devised a new training procedure, one that emphasized language ability, imagination, imitation, verbal rehearsal, and verbal instructions in addition to learning by association and learning by reward. The results obtained with normal children exceeded our most optimistic expectations. The average child of normal intelligence required less than half a day of training. Within three or four hours of intensive training, the young child had learned to toilet himself, was motivated to do so, and, like the retarded adult, had taken a giant step toward feeling independent and in control of his own destiny.

The story did not end with this rapid method of

training normal children. We asked ourselves whether the new features of the procedure for normal children might not also be useful for some of those who are retarded. We found that they were. Many mildly retarded children could use the language-dependent parts of the new procedure and could thereby be trained in less than a day.

We had come full circle. In an attempt to elevate retarded adults to more normal functioning, we had devised an effective procedure for teaching them independence in toileting. Extension of the approach to normal children was successful, but required many changes in technique. These changes, in turn, proved useful when the training method was applied to retarded children.

No single theoretical orientation is followed exclusively. The procedure borrows heavily from the many different approaches to children. We have utilized the psychoanalytic emphasis on the possible effect of harsh toilet training on later personality by making the experience a pleasant one. We have taken advantage of the medical knowledge about toilet training by not advising training until the child is physically ready and free of medical problems. We have acknowledged the importance of Pavlovian learning by ensuring the association of sphincter relaxation with the potty-chair stimuli. We have incorporated the role of operant learning by arranging for many types of reinforcers to follow the desired responses. We have included imitation and social influence by use of a doll that wets and by making the training a social experience. The new method is not an application of any one theory of child training, but rather a combination of the procedures suggested by the many different approaches to children. No "gimmick" or gadget causes the rapid learning. The child learns so fast because we have used so many factors to make learning pleasant, simple, and exciting.

The attitude of mothers toward the new toilet-training procedure has been a surprise. One after another, mothers have expressed delight that "at last" someone was doing something about a major problem of child rearing. The frequency of this expression of gratitude indicates that toilet training is a major problem for most mothers and children, and that the magnitude of the problem was not fully appreciated until a solution was developed.

As important as the new method is for mothers, the major concern was the child. Our objective was to make the toilet-training phase of a child's life the most pleasant experience he had. Spanking and anger were explicitly excluded. We believe that we succeeded in our efforts. During the training, the child was loved, praised, hugged, attended to, and made the center of loving attention. The typical result was that the child smiled, laughed, listened eagerly, and reacted enthusiastically. Typically, at the end of training, he was filled with pride and a sense of accomplishment that he was eagerly sharing with his parents and friends. This increased happiness of the child is the most gratifying aspect of our efforts.

Toilet Training
in Less Than a Day

CHAPTER 1

Current Concerns About Toilet Training: Letters From Mothers

Help!—36 months

I have a 3-year-old son who is partially urine-trained but who will never make a bowel movement on the potty—only in his pants. He has attended a Montessori nursery school for six months, thereby observing other children using the toilet, but to no avail. Help! I have been a working mother, and neither I nor strangers have had any luck. I am no longer working and still have no luck.

At Our Wits' End—47 months

My husband and I have two sons, aged 4 years next month and 2½ years. Both are bright children, but neither one is toilet-trained. Our main problem is with the 4-year-old son. We have tried everything we can think of to train him, but to no avail. He cries, screams, and fights whenever we try to put him on a potty chair or toilet. This occurs with both urination and defecation. He has never urinated in a toilet, and the only time he has had a bowel movement on one was when he had diarrhea and was not able to "hold back" having the B.M. We are at our wits' end. We have also tried putting him in training pants, but he won't even keep them on. He is not the least bit uncomfortable with soiled diapers and would wear the same one all day long if I didn't change him; in fact, many times he even resists my trying to put a clean diaper on him.

Frustrating Him and Me—38 months

I have a little boy, age 38 months. At the age of 2 he trained himself on the bowel-movement cycle. My problem is, he will not train as far as the urinating problem is concerned. I have had him in training pants on three different occasions. I leave him in the training pants for about two weeks and then I find myself frustrating him and me. He seems to be able to hold his urine for only about one-half hour in duration. At this time I have him back in Pampers. I spoke to my pediatrician and he said to leave him alone, but at this point and at his age I feel it is about time he was trained.

He Positively Will Not—32 months

I have two children—a 32-month-old boy and an 11-month-old daughter. I started training my son, Johnny, when he became 24 months old. To date he will be cooperative and urinate in the potty most of the time when I sit him on it. But he hardly ever tells me beforehand when he has to urinate, so I haven't placed him in training pants. My son positively will not release his bowels while sitting on the potty. He waits until he is up walking around. I never punish him about this, but try to convince him it is "big" to do his messes in the potty, and ask him to tell me beforehand the next time he must go. But no luck. I try to be optimistic about it and hope "maybe tomorrow"!!

Tried Everything—42 months

We have a 3½-year-old boy and we are getting nowhere with him and have tried everything.

Always in His Pants—54 months

We are having a problem with our 4½-year-old son. He will not have a bowel movement on a toilet. He has always done it in his pants. He is the youngest child, with a brother and sister. I started toilet-training him at 2 years and it was a complete failure. He refused to go, and after staying dry all night he would hold it all morning and not go until I put him down for an afternoon nap. We moved to another state shortly before he was 3 years old, and we were here two weeks when he discovered he could wet standing up, and that was that; no more problems there. He will start school next fall, and we're really concerned regarding this. We have tried everything and nothing has worked.

Wants No Part of Potty Training—40 months

We are really having a problem with our boy. He is now 3 years and 4 months. He wants no part of potty training. I do not believe in forcing a child, and we have tried all different ways—reading to him, bragging, coaxing, rewards—but he wants no part of it. He just has a fit if we put training pants on him. At times he will go, but not a B.M. He has a temper, and we really believe he is just being stubborn. He also doesn't care if he has dirty pants or wet ones. He is average intelligence, if not a little bit above, we have been told. He has done many things very early in life. In fact, he is one that has to do *everything* himself except for the potty training.

Unsuccessful Trying of Rewards and Punishment—36 months

My son, the eighth of nine children, is 3 years old and still is not toilet-trained, day or night. I

17

have been unsuccessful trying rewards and punishment. Since there are older children in the house, he is very verbal and above average in intelligence, having been able to read since he was 2 years old. My youngest daughter is 14 months old, but I cannot say he has regressed since she was born because he was never truly toilet-trained.

Not Looking Forward to It—16 months
My son is only 16 months old, so I still have some time before I have to start the training process. I'm not looking forward to training. Will my attitude influence my son? My husband is so anxious for our son to be trained, but I'm the one who has to do so.

For Nearly Eight Months I Have Been Trying—32 months
I have a very gentle, sweet, and most of the time cooperative 2-year-8-month-old little girl. She appears to be bright. She walked and talked at an early age. She knows her alphabet. She can recognize numbers and letters, and she can identify simple three- or four-letter words. She sounds like the original wonder baby, almost. She would be wonderful if I could only toilet-train her. For nearly eight months I have been trying to toilet-train her. Why is she so uncooperative and/or hostile? I thought I knew all the theories on toilet training— either taught to me in nursing school or acquired through baby-training manuals or advised by fellow mothers who have better luck than I have had.

Tried Everything I Could Think of—30 months
I have a little girl 2½ years of age. I have been

18

trying for months. I believe she was about 18 or 20 months old when I first started to try and potty-train her, and she is not trained yet. She does very well with the wetting on the potty, but she absolutely will not have a bowel movement on the potty. Either she will sit and cry or she will say she is done, and that is usually when I find her starting to potty. Then I have her sit, and when I get her up in five or ten minutes, I find she has a bowel movement in her panties. She tries to and does hold back. When she was much younger, she used to break out on her bottom very bad, and she was to the point that her bottom was raw, and we used to tell her if she would only potty, her bottom wouldn't be this way. I have training pants for her and that hasn't worked. I have gotten little silk panties and that hasn't worked. My husband and I went on vacation for a week and left her with my sister-in-law and she tried. She has two girls, 11 and 9, and I thought she would have success, and she said she never has seen anything like her. She says she tried everything she could think of. I have also tried spanking and that didn't work. We have told her that she smells bad and no one wants to be around her when she does this. We have tried the big toilet instead of her potty chair. I have ignored her and that didn't work. I have tried everything I can think of; my pediatrician told me she would do it when she was ready and to ignore her, but I am at wit's end trying to find the method. We also have an 8-month-old little boy, but we tried before he came along.

He Won't Even Try—30 months
My son is 2½ years old and won't even try.

19

I Will Never Be Able to Train Her—25 months

I have a 25-month-old daughter whom I have been trying to potty-train for three months. She is bright but acts lazy and will not always cooperate. I don't know what to do. I'm afraid I will never be able to train her.

To Go by Himself on His Own Is Impossible— 30 months

I have a 2½-year-old boy who refuses to go potty for me. He would just as soon go into another room and wet or dirty his pants. He will go potty when I remind him he has to go, but to go by himself on his own is impossible. I also have a 2-month-old baby girl, but this was occurring before she was born.

Don't Know What Else I Should Do—30 months

My child is 2½ and couldn't care less about the potty. I don't believe in forcing him to use it, but don't know what else I should do.

Still Wets and Dirties Her Panties—5 years

I have a grandchild 5 years old who still wets and dirties her panties.

Not Toilet-Broke—6 years

I have a son almost 6 years old. He is not retarded. He has been checked for this. He has been checked closely by a pediatrician and a urologist. They can find no physical reason for his not being toilet-broke. I have tried everything I could think of. I am at my wit's end. I need help badly on breaking him of this. I need this help desperately.

Boys Are Harder to Train—24 months

My son is just 2, and I am ready to train him. As the mother of three girls, and with everyone telling me how much harder it is to train boys, I am quite anxious to learn your method.

Couldn't Care Less—36 months

I have a son 3 years old who couldn't care less about being toilet-trained.

I Am Desperate—24 and 36 months

I've got three children ages 3, 2, and 1, with another due any day. I've been trying to train the two oldest ones for months on end now. First, I tried everything I know of, such as praise and presents. Nothing seems to work. I am desperate— otherwise I wouldn't have sent you this letter.

Smart but Stubborn—30 months

My daughter is 2½ and I am having a problem training her. She will sit on the potty, but she will not go in it. She is quite smart for her age, but I think stubbornness is her problem.

She Knows How, but . . . —24 months

My little girl is 2 years old, and I have a 3-month-old baby. I am at my wit's end with my little girl: she knows how and sometimes does use the potty (especially anywhere but at home), but she so often just wets in her pants, time after time. What am I to do to help her use the potty *every time*? I also need to know your method for when my little boy is ready to be trained.

21

Sits for Over Three Hours—18 months

I have an 18-month-old son who just refuses to be trained. Just when I think we are making progress, he gets worse again. He has told me for some time when his bowels have to move, and when I'm in the shower he will go to the potty himself. Just recently he hasn't been letting me know this. When I know that he has to urinate I put him on the potty, and often he sits for over three hours before having any success. He will hold back just as long as he possibly can. Yet when he does have success, he is so proud of himself—this is what I can't understand. We reward him with hugs, praise, and candy. He has done everything earlier than the norm, and we have felt for a long time that he was ready to be trained. We will soon be traveling overseas and are most anxious to begin training before we go. It has now become such a battle to make him sit on the potty, and I feel that this isn't good for him psychologically. It really has us worried. He is so stubborn. Can these months of unsuccessful training be erased in order to start over with your method? I really don't know what to try next, and the constant battles and frustration worry me no end.

I Am a New Mother—3 months

I am a new mother and am very much interested in toilet training. My baby is 3 months old and I will be faced with this problem shortly.

A Mother's Dilemma: Patience vs. Self-Sacrifice

The above comments by mothers describe the typical and serious problems caused when their child is not toilet-trained. All children must learn to toilet themselves. Yet until recently, no method of toilet training has been demonstrated to hasten the age at which the child is trained. Since special problems are often created for the child and for the parent by common methods of training, psychologists and physicians have almost universally advised mothers not to pressure their child. This advice to the mother to let the child train himself is justified as a method of preventing the severe strains and stress of procedures that have not been found to make a difference. The mother finds herself in a dilemma. On the one hand, she faces great demands on her time, energy, and patience as long as her child is still wetting and soiling himself. But she is told she must not remedy the situation lest she create even more serious problems.

What If I Don't Train?

Skin Irritations

What are the disadvantages of waiting until a child is ready to toilet-train himself? First, medical problems can occur in the form of soreness, redness, and diaper rash because of the wet diapers. Medicating powders and lotions probably will become a routine, either as a preventive measure or to provide temporary relief.

How Much Time Is Taken in Changing Diapers?

The time required of the mother is substantial. The typical 2-year-old child wets or soils himself about seven or eight times a day, thereby requiring about seven or eight diaper changes. Each change of diapers requires that the mother obtain a fresh

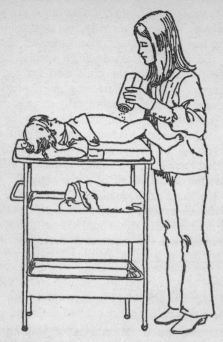

Diaper rash can produce a sore bottom.

diaper, remove the wet diaper, wash or wipe off or powder the child, put on a fresh diaper and dispose of the wet diaper, and clean up any floor stains. Bowel movements will often require much longer than ten minutes, but an approximate average for the entire episode from detection to completion is about ten minutes. When this duration is multiplied by the number of changes per week, the time required is about nine hours per week. Add to this duration the time spent in washing and drying the diapers and we realize that the mother of an untrained child spends the equivalent of one-fourth of a full-time work week simply in changing diapers. If a child remains untrained for one year after he might have been trained, the mother has spent the equivalent of three months of full-time employment unnecessarily disposing of urine and feces and changing stained clothing. For mothers who have no interests or responsibilities other than the care of one child, this time requirement may be bearable. But the typical mother who has other responsibilities and recreational desires—who enjoys reading, visiting friends, watching television, listening to the radio, playing with her other children, or interacting with her husband—will find this role of diaper changer to be a serious interruption of her personal joys. Should she have several children, the care of the other children will suffer, as will also the household duties and her ability to perform outside employment, since she will often find that nursery schools will not accept untrained children.

How Expensive Is It to Use Diapers?

The expense incurred by the need for changing diapers is not excessive, yet is very real to those who must be budget-conscious. Assuming seven diaper changes per day, the current price of disposable diapers will result in an expense of about $200 per year, which is also the approximate cost of a commercial diaper service. This amount may be reduced if one uses a washing machine, but then the time spent is even greater. If a child remains untrained unnecessarily for one year, about $200, or its equivalent in time, will have been spent unnecessarily.

*Will My Child and I Get Along Better
If I Don't Try to Train Him?*

As important as time, money, and effort are, the major concern of many mothers is the nature of the parent–child relationship. The reports of mothers indicate that as a child grows older, the lack of toilet training causes progressively greater strains and tensions. The untrained child imposes an over-dependent state on himself and the mother. The mother cannot leave the child without concern about his wetting himself. She cannot leave him

Old training methods aren't always fun.

with friends easily, or with baby-sitters. Long trips require careful planning for diaper changes and disposal. The child remains in a dependent state that encourages dependence on the mother for other activities, such as dressing. The child sometimes learns to soil himself deliberately as a means of obtaining attention. The mother often receives criticism from the father, relatives, friends, and neighbors, who view the lack of toilet training as evidence of her general incompetence as a mother. When the mother discovers that her child has "wet again," she is not likely to exhibit gleeful delight, but rather to communicate her despair and disappointment to the child, who must surely feel that he is no longer a source of joy and happiness.

In the face of this effort, expense, time required, dependency, and personal/social strain, many mothers ignore the advice of their family doctor or child psychologists. They decide that the inconvenience of changing diapers all day for several months to come is too great, and they try to train their child.

What If I Do Train?

The Old Method of Training

In the most commonly used toilet-training procedure, the mother seats her child on a potty chair at those times in the day when he has usually urinated. The child is required to remain in the chair, often strapped in place, until urination occurs—which may require an hour or more, during which time the mother tries to remain with the child but must be absent when other duties demand her attention. If the child has urinated, she may praise or reward the child and allow him to leave the potty. This

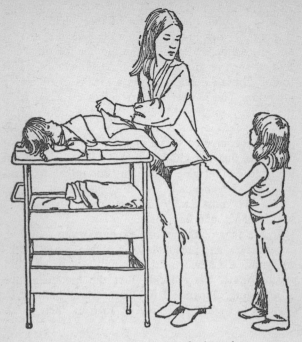

What happens if you don't train.

detection usually occurs several seconds or minutes after urination began. If the child takes too long, she pleads and coaxes. If he wets himself after he has left the potty chair, she may well scold or spank him.

Problems During Training With the Old Method

The old method of toilet training presents many problems. The procedure requires considerable time on the part of the mother. She must undress the child, seat him on the chair, remain with him for an

28

extended period, dress him again, and empty the potty if he has urinated. This scene is repeated every two or three hours every day for months or even for a year or two. Unless the mother has almost unlimited time, accidents will continue to occur because of the child's need to urinate at unscheduled moments or because of the mother's understandable inability to predict when he has the desire. Even when the child has learned to tell her when he must urinate, she must interrupt what she is doing to assist him, and accidents will occur when she is preoccupied or not easily available. Some children become fearful of the potty chair and refuse to sit on it or even to enter the bathroom where it is located. Some children refuse to wear training pants or to undress and dress themselves for toileting. Some children hold their urine while seated on the potty chair, only to urinate shortly after arising. The continuing occurrence of accidents often irritates the mother so severely that she begins to nag, scold, and shame the child and begins to use physical punishment. Faced with these punishments for not achieving something he has not learned, the child may begin to engage in temper tantrums, become deceitful and secretive in concealing his wet pants, and learn to fear his mother. The old toilet-training effort often creates severe parent–child conflicts.

Problems After Training With the Old Method
Even when the child has learned by the old method to urinate only upon being seated on the chair, problems still often arise. Many of these problems are caused by the passivity and dependence created by the old method of training. The child usually continues to wait for the mother to remind

Be prepared to be interrupted if you have taught your child to tell you when he needs to be put on the potty.

him to toilet, to take him to the potty chair, to undress and dress him, and to empty the potty bowl. Even when the child has learned to communicate his desire to urinate, the mother must be prepared to interrupt immediately whatever she is doing to assist and accompany the child. Other problems that commonly arise from the old method are that the child continues to ask for approval for toileting himself, continues to require that the mother be present when he sits on the potty chair, still has occasional accidents when the mother is not easily available, continues to have bowel accidents, and may begin wetting himself again when a new baby arrives or when the family moves to a new home.

To Train or Not to Train

The problems caused by the old method of training, and the problems persisting even after that type of training, are often as great as the problems of having the child untrained. Neither solution has been satisfactory.

CHAPTER 2

A New Method and Its Evaluation

How Did the New Method Come About?

We have seen that major problems exist for both the parent and the child if the child is left untrained, but that equally great problems are caused by the old method of training. Until very recently, no specific advice could be given to mothers as to how to improve the training procedure, since no improved training procedure had yet been developed. Very recently, however, learning specialists have become interested in toilet training and have developed procedures that do work better and have been shown in scientific comparisons to be superior to the usual method. The authors are themselves learning specialists who have been developing improved toilet-training procedures and have developed a new procedure that eliminates or minimizes the major problems in the old method. At the present time, the new procedure appears to have more advantages than the old methods. Mothers no longer need to refrain from training because of their fear of the problems created by training.

Has This Method Been Tested?

A formal study was conducted by the authors to evaluate the new training method (see References: Foxx and Azrin, 1973a). About two hundred children have been trained by the new method, one-sixth of whom were in the formal study.

What Type of Children Were Used in the Evaluation of This Method?

The children ranged from 20 months of age to over 4 years of age. Both sexes were included. Some of the children could speak well; others used no more than one or two words. Some had repeatedly failed to learn by procedures used by their parents, relatives, neighbors, and "Head Start" nursery-school teachers, whereas others received the new method as their first attempt at training. Some were characterized by their parents as "little devils" and stubborn, others as "angels" and cooperative. Some of the children seemed very alert and attentive; others, slow and indifferent. Some children had no brothers or sisters; others had as many as four other children present in the family, one of whom was sometimes an untrained baby or a similarly untrained twin. Income levels of the parents ranged from a welfare subsistence to suburban affluence. The mothers had as low an education level as grade school or as high as graduate university degrees. The fathers' occupations varied from unemployed or unskilled laborers to physicians, psychologists, educators, ministers, counselors, and artists. In some homes, no father was present. In other homes, the mother worked full or part time, leaving the child in the care of baby-sitters, relatives, or neighbors. Concern about the lack of training varied from simple curiosity as to whether training was possible to frantic desperation. Typically, the father felt it was the mother's problem. Many mothers and fathers were openly skeptical. A few children had been partly trained, in that the child would reliably urinate in the potty chair when he was placed on it but not otherwise.

The results of the field test with the various children were impressive.

Speed of Training by the New Method

The average child required less than four hours to be trained to toilet himself completely independently without assistance or a reminder. Some children were trained in as little as thirty minutes. The longest time required by any child was two days (fourteen training hours). Girls trained slightly faster (by one-half hour) than boys. Older children, over the age of 26 months, tended to train faster, in about two and one-half hours, than children younger than 26 months, who averaged about five hours.

Completeness of Training by the New Method

When a child is described by a neighbor as being toilet-trained, she probably means that her child will urinate in the potty chair when the child is taken to the chair, undressed, and seated on the chair. After urinating, the child is then dressed by the mother, and the mother disposes of the urine. In the new method, the child carries out all these activities completely by himself even when the mother is absent. The child does not wait for a reminder from the parent; he decides by himself when to urinate. The child does not wait for his mother to accompany him; he goes to the potty chair alone from any location in the home. He lowers his pants without assistance or reminder and sits on the potty chair until he urinates and remains seated until he has completed the act. If the child is a girl or if the child has a bowel movement, the child would also have wiped himself or herself. He then arises by himself and pulls up his pants without assistance. Then he removes the potty from the chair and carries it to the toilet, taking great care not to spill the contents. He empties the pot into the adult toilet stool and flushes the toilet. Finally, he carries the empty pot back to the potty chair and reinserts it in its proper place. No effort, supervision, or time is required from the mother after a child is trained by this new method. The child is not simply toilet-trained; we can describe him more accurately as being toilet-educated.

Success Rate with the New Method

All children who were 20 months of age or over, who were at least somewhat responsive to instructions, and whose parents desired the training were trained, without exception. No attempt was made to train children who had not yet learned to respond to their parents' instructions or children who were under 20 months of age. With the only two children who were not completely trained by the new method, the father was actively opposed to training. These two exceptions indicate that the father should be convinced of the desirability of having his child toilet-trained before training is attempted. Probably the best method of changing his attitude is to have him take the responsibility for changing the diapers.

Benefits After Training with the New Method

After training by the new method, many benefits occurred for the parent and the child. No harmful effects have been observed. Typically, the child was now delighted with his newly acquired skill. Many

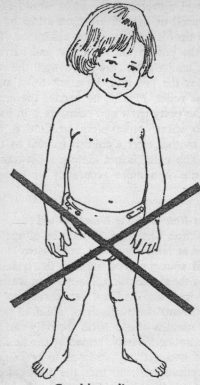

Good-bye, diapers.

mothers reported that this independence generalized
to other activities, such as the child's feeding himself and dressing himself; that the child's personality
had improved, since he now felt more independent;
that he was now very much aware of his personal
appearance; that the relationship to the mother had
changed from avoidance to pride; and that the child
was now more responsive to the mother's instruc-

tions. An unexpected bonus was that one-third of the children also stopped wetting their beds. The mothers, as we might expect, reported that the benefits to themselves were equally substantial. Many stated that they were no longer impatient with and ashamed of their child and now had ample time for their personal interests and other duties. Most important, many mothers reported that they now viewed their child as a source of pride and pleasure rather than as a source of interruptions and drudgery. The parent–child conflicts that were caused by the lack of training or by the old method of training seemed to have been solved by the new training procedure.

Pleasantness of the New Training Experience

All of the children seemed to enjoy the training experience. The reason for their pleasure was probably that the procedure stresses praise and approval. During the training the child had the undivided attention of the adult trainer, who was constantly guiding, praising, approving, and giving demonstrations. The child was never taught more than one easily handled step at a time, and disapproval was given only upon an accident, which occurred only once or twice for most children. At the end of the training, the child was usually proudly and gleefully displaying his newly developed independence to all who were interested.

Follow-Up of the New Training Procedure

For several months after the new training procedure had been used, the mothers reported regularly on their children's progress. All children maintained the benefit of the training for as long as these follow-up reports were obtained, which has been as long as two years. For the average child, accidents were reduced by 90 percent on the very first day after training, by 95 percent by the third day, and by 99 percent by the end of one week. The rare accidents that occurred thereafter were usually the result of understandable complications such as illness or overly tight clothing.

CHAPTER 3

General Teaching Plan

Teaching Objectives

The overall objective is to teach your child to toilet himself with the same independence as an adult and without the need for reminders, continued praise, or assistance. To achieve this objective, he should be taught the specific skills of approaching the potty chair and seating himself on it, to lower and raise his pants by himself, to sit quietly on the potty chair until he urinates, to wipe himself after pottying when needed, to empty the pot into a toilet stool, to flush the toilet stool, to return the pot to the chair, and to be motivated to potty himself before the urgent need arises.

Teaching Aids and Supplies

Before starting, obtain the teaching aids and supplies that you will need. The teaching aids that are needed are a hollow doll that wets and a well-designed potty chair of the type that is easily emptied. Among the necessary teaching supplies are a variety of tasty drinks; candies and other treats; and several pairs of loosely fitting training pants. Chapter 4 describes these materials and supplies in detail. A list of these supplies and several other reminder sheets you will need can be found in Chapter 7.

Instructional Procedures and Rationale

The more a child urinates during the training, the greater will be the opportunities to teach him to do it correctly. Therefore, you will give the child all he wants to drink in order to increase his desire to urinate.

Since distractions interfere with learning, you will select an area of the home where the instruction can be carried out in privacy and without distraction or interruption by other family members or by other activities.

To accustom your child to using the potty chair, you will give him repeated practice in walking to the chair. At the start of these chair-approach trials, you will teach him to lower and raise his pants himself.

Since urination is more likely in a relaxed state, you will teach him to sit quietly once he is seated on the chair.

Since the child has limited language, you will give very brief and simple instructions about each small action.

To avoid total reliance on his limited language, you will use the doll that wets to teach by imitation, demonstrating how the doll potties herself correctly.

A useful aid to learning is to have the student try to teach another student. You will use this aid by having your child teach the doll how to potty.

Another method of avoiding reliance on the limited language is gentle manual guidance, which you will provide whenever your child does not respond to an instruction.

To motivate your child to potty correctly, you will show your approval for his new skills. For maximum motivation, you will use many types of approval, including praise, hugging, and rewards. You will give them frequently and enthusiastically and immediately after each action, especially upon the child's urinating in the pot and properly disposing of its contents.

To convey the general social importance of tidiness, you will teach your child that additional approval awaits him from all of the persons who are important to him. You will do this by continually informing him of how these persons will react to each correct pottying action.

You wish to stress the attitude of personal cleanliness. The act of pottying is the means, but only the means, of demonstrating this attitude. Accordingly, you will continually communicate to your child your pleasure at his cleanly state. Indeed, once he has demonstrated that he can perform all of the pottying actions, the approval is given exclusively for remaining dry. Similarly, the reminders and instructions to potty are progressively reduced and eliminated entirely once your child has shown that he can potty without a reminder. This independence education has also been applied to the learning of the specific pottying acts by a progressive reduction in the degree of manual guidance.

The child will have accidents during training and occasionally even after training, and must be shown parental disapproval and concern. To show this concern in a constructive manner, and simultaneously to continue this education toward personal responsibility, you will require him to change his wet clothing himself when he has an accident and to practice the varying pottying actions. This constructive reaction to accidents avoids the usual practice of angry nagging, scolding, or physical punishment and allows the instructional atmosphere to be pleasant and approving.

Why This Method Is So Rapid

The method is so rapid because it includes so many of the factors that are known to speed up learning. As is described above, these factors include learning without distraction, increasing the frequency of urination opportunities, practice in walking to the potty chair, practice in the required dressing skills, learning to relax before urinating, learning by imitation, learning by teaching, learning by manual guidance, increasing the motivation to be trained, and teaching the general attitude of personal cleanliness, as well as the additional factors noted. Ordinary toilet training includes only some of these experiences and only some of the time that they are needed. When the mother, following this method, arranges for all of these experiences to take place all of the times that they are needed, learning is easier for the child and consequently occurs more rapidly. If any of the procedures are omitted, the training will not be as easy for your child and will require a longer duration.

CHAPTER 4

How to Train

Preliminary Considerations and Procedures

What Age?

If your child is 20 months old, he is probably capable of being toilet-trained by this new method. Bear in mind that children vary somewhat in their rate of physical and mental development and bladder control. Accordingly, your child may be ready at a slightly earlier age, which may be as young as 18 months. You can give three simple tests for determining readiness: one for Bladder Control, one for Physical Development, and the third one for Instructional Readiness.

Bladder Control

1) Does my child urinate a good deal at one time rather than dribbling throughout the day? 2) Does he often stay dry for several hours? 3) Does he appear to know he is about to urinate as indicated by his facial expressions or by special postures he adopts? If he does all three, he is aware of his bladder sensations and has enough bladder control to begin training. If he does only the first two, he may still be ready for training, since not all children give this visible indication of their desire to urinate.

Physical Readiness

Does he have enough finger and hand coordination to pick up objects easily? Does he walk from

Showing Mommy that you can follow instructions.

room to room easily and without the need for assistance? If he does, he is sufficiently developed physically.

Instructional Readiness

To determine if your child has sufficient social responsiveness and understanding, ask him to carry out the following ten actions: Ask him to show you (point to) 1) his nose, 2) his eyes, 3) his mouth, 4) his hair. Ask him 5) to sit down on a chair, 6) to stand up, 7) to walk with you to a particular place, such as another room, 8) to imitate you in a simple task, such as playing patty-cake, 9) to bring you a familiar object, such as one of his toys, 10) to place one familiar object with another—for example, "Put the dolly in the wagon." If he carries out eight of these ten instructions, he should be considered intellectually ready for training.

If He Does Not Pass the Readiness Tests

Most children over 20 months of age seem to be able to pass all three of these tests.

If your child does not pass the test for Bladder Control or for Physical Development, you should wait until he has developed more coordination and more bladder control. Initial bladder control and physical coordination are very much a matter of simple maturation.

Insufficient Language Development

If your child has not passed the Instructional Readiness Test, the reason may be that he does not yet have enough language development; he cannot understand the meaning of many simple words. If lack of understanding seems to be his problem in following the instructions, you may be able to teach him rather than waiting until he is older. The important words are PLACE words such as "here," "there," "down," "up"; BODY words such as "hand," "foot," "legs," and "arms"; IDENTITY words such as "you," "me," and "her,"; and TOILET words, such as "potty," "diaper," "pants," "wet," and "dry." However, if your child has the usual amount of interaction with other verbal children or adults, he will learn these simple words in time with no need for special language instruction. Once he has learned the meaning of the above words, teach him to follow the simple instructions in the Instructional Readiness Test. Once he has learned to follow these instructions, and if he has passed the other two tests, you can proceed to toilet-train him.

Stubbornness

If your child has not passed the Instructional Readiness Test, the reason may be that he is stubborn and not that he has slow language development. You know that he understands what you have said, but he refuses to carry out your instructions. If stubbornness is the problem, you cannot depend on advancing age to solve it. The other problems— of bladder control, coordination, and language development—are usually solved by simple waiting. Stubbornness, on the other hand, may very well increase with age. Until this general stubbornness is overcome, you should not attempt to toilet-train. If your child refuses to follow instructions about actions that he has already learned, he is not likely to follow instructions about actions he has not yet mastered.

Teaching the Stubborn Child to Follow Instructions

Before you start toilet-training a child who is stubborn, you should first teach him to follow your instructions. This manual contains many rules for ensuring cooperation by a child in learning to toilet himself. You should read through the manual to learn these rules. Apply these rules to teaching your child to follow your instructions in general before trying to apply these rules to toilet training. Some of these rules are 1) Give instructions only when you are next to the child, 2) Obtain the child's attention before giving an instruction, 3) Provide gentle manual guidance within one second or two after an instruction if the child does not start following the instruction, 4) Give enthusiastic approval as soon as an instruction is followed, 5) Do not give a second instruction until the first one has been completed, 6) Do not allow a tantrum to deter you from seeing to it that the instruction is followed. Use these rules to teach your child to carry out your instructions regarding his general activities, such as closing the door after he enters the house, picking up his toys, coming to you when you ask, giving you an object, sitting down, and walking to his bedroom and other such activities when stubbornness has been exhibited. When he does follow these instructions readily, give him the Instructional Readiness Test again. If he passes the test, proceed with toilet training.

Mental Retardation

If your child is mildly retarded and cannot understand instructions easily, you cannot use the new method without making several changes in the method. The needed changes are described in the Appendix on page 177. For children or adults who are extremely retarded, the present method is not applicable. For these individuals, the authors have developed a different procedure, which is described in two publications, Azrin and Foxx, 1971 and Foxx and Azrin, 1973b, both of which are listed in the Reference section at the end of this book.

Pretraining Experiences

Several things can be done while your child is very young to make him ready to be trained at an earlier age. 1) Have your child learn to assist in dressing and undressing himself, especially in lowering and raising his pants. Even if he cannot put on an article of clothing completely unassisted, encourage him to carry out part of the process. For example, in putting on trousers, he may be unable to place his feet through the pant legs, but once you have done that for him, have him pull the pants up to his waist.

2) Allow him to watch you (and his brothers and sisters, if any) and others toilet themselves. While he is watching, point out the various steps such as "Look, I'm going to the toilet; see, now I'm pulling my pants down." Even have him assist by flushing the toilet for you.

3) Teach him the meaning of the words that will be used later in toilet training, such as "potty chair," "pants," "wet," "dry," "sit down," "stand up," "empty." Also, teach the words you prefer for pottying, such as "urination," "pee," "pee-pee," "wee-wee," "defecation," "poo-poo," and "B.M."

4) Teach him to cooperate in following your instructions. Some guidelines are: When you direct

him to do something of which he is capable, do not allow the instruction to go unfulfilled. Praise him when he starts to try to carry out the directions. Do not allow a temper tantrum to discourage you when he is reluctant to do something that you have instructed him to do.

Who Should Do the Training?

Traditionally, the mother has had the responsibility to do the training. However, anyone who has a good relationship with the child can serve as the teacher: the father, older brother or sister, babysitter, nursery-school teacher, day-care teacher, or a friend of the family. If you have any doubts about your ability to be objective during the training, you may wish to consider asking a neighbor to train your child. You, in turn, could repay the favor by training her child. The most important consideration is that the trainer be very conscientious in carrying out the training procedure.

Previous Attempts to Train

Do not attempt to use the old method of toilet training before you use the new method. The reason for this advice is that your child may develop a strong dislike for pottying himself if he has experienced failure. Because of these earlier failures, more time will be needed to learn, and training may require considerably more than one day. If such failures have occurred, training may be more effective if conducted by the father or a friend who was not involved in the previous attempt.

Medical or Physical Problems

For a very small proportion of children, a physical condition may interfere with their ability to control their bladders and bowels voluntarily. If you suspect that your child has any physical problem that might affect his ability to toilet, obtain medical advice before beginning training. Some warning signs of medical problems are that the child urinates very frequently throughout the day with few periods of dryness, or that urination or defecation is painful. Postpone training if your child has diarrhea or constipation or is not feeling well. If your child has epilepsy or has seizures, you should not give excessive fluids. If your child has diabetes, he may require candies, treats, and drinks that are sugar-free. If your child is allergic to specific foods or drinks, you should use nonallergenic substitutes for the suggested ones. See your physician if you suspect any complications that might arise from the foods or the drinks or any other aspect of training.

Where to Train

Training is usually conducted most conveniently in the kitchen. The kitchen floor is usually designed to withstand spills or wettings, the necessary drinks can be kept cold, ice is available in the kitchen refrigerator, and a variety of snack items is usually stored there. If the kitchen is extremely small and confining, select some other room whose floor is not carpeted and will not stain so readily.

Snacks and Treats

Small snack items are needed—such as sugar-coated cereal, potato chips, candy, corn chips, celery or carrot sticks, fruit slices, ice cream or sherbet—as part of your demonstration of approval

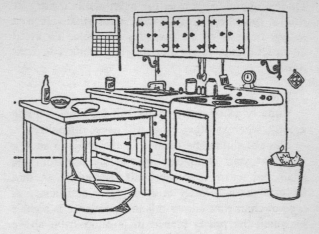

Toilet training in the kitchen.

of your child for pottying correctly and for remaining dry. Since you wish to use these snacks to communicate your special pleasure, choose snack items that you know he likes best and considers to be a rare treat. When possible, carry these items in a pocket or apron, so that you will have them readily available when you need them.

Drinks

A variety of drinks should be available for use at the start of training. These drinks will be used as a reward, just as the snacks are, and should therefore be highly prized. The drinks will also serve to create a strong desire in your child to urinate, thereby providing many more urinations and more opportunities to teach your child how to potty correctly. The more your child likes the drinks you give him, the more he will drink and the more potty trials will be available for instruction. Favorites for most children are soft drinks, punches, fruit juices, and milk. Have a supply of each of his favorites available. To avoid an upset stomach, do not use both milk and fruit juices.

What Type of Potty Chair?

Some types of potty chairs will facilitate training greatly, whereas other types will cause difficulties.

The pot should be located in the chair in such a way that your child can remove the pot from the chair and return it to the chair very easily, so that he can potty himself without your assistance. A type of chair that allows this independence is a chair in which the pot is placed in position from above rather than being inserted from the back of the chair. Several such chairs are now available. If you do not use a chair with an easily removable pot, you must empty the pot for your child and should not require him to do so.

A desirable feature of a potty chair is that the chair automatically provide a signal to you at the moment your child urinates in the pot. Since you should give your child approval as soon as he urinates in the pot, this urine-signaling feature will tell you when to show that approval. Potty chairs that provide this automatic signaling of urination have been developed recently. Do not be overly concerned and do not delay training if you are unable to obtain a urine-signaling chair. Training can be completed just as quickly with chairs of other types if you watch your child very closely while he is on the pot and give him approval as soon as he starts to urinate in the pot.

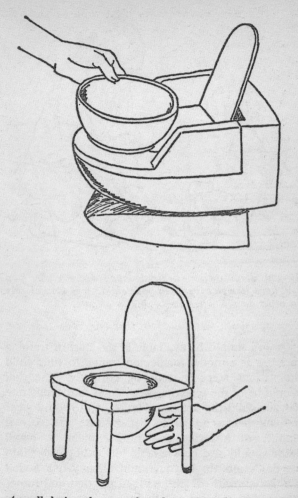

A well-designed potty chair has a pot that is removed from the top. Old-fashioned potty chairs have a pot that is removed from the back of the chair.

If you don't own a urine-signaling potty chair, you will have to watch between your child's legs very closely in order to tell when he begins to urinate.

Doll

A doll should be available at the start of training to serve as a model for demonstrating to your child the various steps in toileting correctly. The doll should be of the type that wets, so as to demonstrate to your child the act of urination, and should wear training pants, so as to demonstrate the correct manner of lowering and raising them. A small bottle should also be available for putting water into the doll's mouth. If your child already has a doll of this type with which he plays, use that doll rather than a different one. Dolls that wet are commonly available from department stores and large mail-order houses.

Friends-Who-Care List

When you will be praising your child during training, you will be telling him not only that you are pleased but also that others too will be pleased. To facilitate this, use the Friends-Who-Care procedure. Make up a list of all the persons and friends your child admires, such as Daddy, his big brothers and sisters, his grandfather, his aunt, the mailman, and the baby-sitter. Also include fictional persons whom he admires, such as Santa Claus and television characters such as the Flintstones, Captain Kangaroo, and the *Sesame Street* characters. You will use this list during training to remind yourself to mention all of these persons.

Eliminate Distractions

You wish to have your home free of distractions; otherwise you and your child will not be able to concentrate on the instruction. Turn off radios and television sets in the house. Remove all toys and games from the kitchen training area. If the telephone rings, ignore it, or tell the caller you will call back later. Plan a lunch and dinner that can be prepared within a few minutes, or better still, prepare the meals before you start training. If callers arrive at your home, explain your preoccupation and return immediately to your child. Arrange to have brothers or sisters, as well as other adults, out of the house. This may be arranged on a weekend, when the father or a neighbor may care for the children away from the home. Your intent is to give your child your undivided attention, and you should not allow any event to interrupt the interaction.

If another adult, such as the father, or an older child must be present in the house, have him actively assist you in the instruction rather than simply observing. A common problem that arises when two adults are present is that they then spend their time communicating with each other rather than with the child. Often the discussion is not related to the toilet training. If another adult does assist you, have him agree to speak primarily to the child. Any comments to you should be concerned with toilet training. Your child may also introduce a topic that is not relevant to training, such as noticing that it is raining, asking where Daddy is, asking about television, or pointing to a flower design on your apron. Do not allow these comments to distract him and you from the training. Instead, redirect his comment by a statement about the importance of his learning to toilet himself.

Naps

If the training takes more than three or four hours for your child, he may require a nap, especially if he is very young. You will probably recognize the usual signals of the need for a nap when he becomes tired and irritable at the time when he usually takes a nap. The nap should be considered as a necessary interruption to the training which you would like to complete quickly. To minimize this interruption, ensure that your child has received a good night's rest, that the nap is postponed slightly if you are almost finished with training, and that the nap is made briefer than usual.

Cloth Training Pants

The child should wear cloth training pants during training. The pants should be several sizes larger than what the child would wear normally, since the larger the pants, the more easily the child will be able to pull them down and up. The pants should be so loose at the waist that they are almost at the size where they might slide down the child's hips. If the waist is too tight, stretch it by pulling the elastic waistband. If stretching does not increase the size sufficiently, clip the waistband with scissors. The legs of the pants should also fit loosely. If they fit too tightly, stretch or clip the leg openings just as you did for the waistband. Once your child has learned during training how to lower and raise these loosely fitting pants, he will be motivated and able to cope with his normal size, which should be given him only after he has remained dry for several days. At least eight pairs of the loose training pants should be ready for use at the start of training.

Training Procedures

Sequence of Procedures

The training procedures are described in detail below. The procedures are arranged to approximate the order in which they are used. Although many procedures are used simultaneously and in various combinations, each procedure is described separately in this chapter. Chapter 6 then describes by an illustrative example of a training day the sequence in which the different procedures are used. This chapter tells you why and how to conduct each procedure. Chapter 6 will teach you how to combine all of the procedures.

When to Use Each Procedure:
Your Child Is Unique

You will use some procedures at regular intervals of time, such as prompting your child to the potty about every fifteen minutes or making the dry-pants inspections every few minutes. Some procedures are used only at the beginning such as the Doll-That-Wets procedure. Other procedures are used almost continuously, such as the instructions and approval, whereas the manual-guidance procedure is used only after an instruction has been given and been found inadequate. All of the procedures are based on your child's actions. For example, the Doll-That-Wets procedure ends when your child is able to teach the doll; the instructions become more general as your child shows he can follow the more detailed instructions; and the approval is deferred until the end of an action once your child has mastered the specific actions. Your child is unique. We recognize this uniqueness by letting his abilities and actions determine when and how long a procedure is to be used. The result is that the instruction is geared to your child and each child will advance at his own rate. In each of the procedural descriptions that follow, rules are given as to how you should change the procedure as your child progresses.

Doll-That-Wets: Learning by Imitation and Learning by Teaching.

Teaching the Doll to Potty Herself

You use the doll that wets to teach your child by imitation what specific actions he should learn in toileting and what types of social approval he can expect to receive for these actions. Have your child guide the doll through the required motions, and have him give approval to the doll for the correct actions. Assist your child by instruction and manual guidance to teach him what to do. Before demon-

Giving the doll a drink.

strating, dress the doll in training pants. Then fill the doll with several ounces of water.

Now tell the child that the doll (use the doll's name if she has one) has to "pee-pee." Then instruct your child to help the doll approach the potty chair, lower her pants, sit on the potty, and remain quietly on the chair. You should assist your child by gently guiding his hands when he has not followed your instructions as to what to do for the doll.

Placing the doll on the potty.

When the doll has been sitting on the potty, tell your child to look between the doll's legs, because she is about to pee-pee. Then cause the doll to wet by squeezing her or by whatever other method is needed for the type of doll you are using. For dif-

Helping the doll to the potty.

Lowering the doll's pants.

ferent types of dolls you may have to tilt the doll,
or pull a homemade plug from the bottom hole.

When the stream of water comes from between
the doll's legs and into the pot, have your child
look at and possibly even feel the water as it falls
into the pot, so that he is sure to be aware of what
has happened. As soon as the doll begins wetting,
encourage your child to praise the doll enthusiastically—"Dolly is a big girl, she goes pee-pee in the
potty"—and to clap his hands, and to pat the doll's
head to show the doll that he shares your great happiness that she has urinated in the pot. At the same
time, direct your child to offer the doll a snack
treat. After your child discovers that the doll can-

61

Placing the doll on the potty.

not eat it, tell him that he can have it if he will be a big boy and go pee-pee in the potty like the dolly. If the child signifies by word or by head nod that he intends to be "a big boy," give him the snack.

Emptying the Potty

Your child should now assist the doll in raising her pants, then set the doll aside for a few minutes. Instruct your child to "help Dolly to empty the pot." Guide your child as he removes the pot from the potty chair and carries it to the household toilet to be emptied. After you have guided him in emptying the pot, have your child hold the pot in one hand

Giving the doll a treat for urinating in the potty.

while you instruct and manually guide him to flush the toilet with his other hand. Do not allow him to release the pot while he is flushing, since he will probably forget to pick up the pot in his excitement. He should flush with the hand he favors in picking up objects. The child is then guided in carrying the pot back to the chair and reinserting it in its proper place. The trainer accompanies the child throughout the trip to and from the bathroom, remaining in close contact with the child so as to be ready to intervene should the plastic pot start to tip.

Importance of Being Dry

After the pot has been put back in place, instruct and guide the child to ask the doll if her pants are

Lifting the pot from the chair.

dry and to feel her pants. Since the pants will be dry, have the child praise the doll and offer her a snack treat. Ask the child if his pants are dry; if so, he is allowed to eat the doll's snack treat for being "a big boy with dry pants." Repeat the same procedure with the drink. Your child should repeat this inspection of the doll's pants two or three more times, spaced a few minutes apart.

Doll Wets Her Pants

After two or three pants checks, distract your child momentarily while you spill some water on the doll's training pants. At the next pants inspection, your child will discover the wet pants. Instruct your child to tell the doll by word or gesture that he is displeased that she has wet her pants. "No, Dolly,

64

On the way to the bathroom to empty the pot's contents.

big girls don't wet their pants." Again, if the child
has not begun talking, ask him if the doll is a baby
—to which he should nod his head. Then instruct
your child to "help the doll practice going to the
potty." Tell him that the doll must practice because
she wet her pants. Also, tell him that, by practicing,
the doll will learn where she should pee-pee. Use
instructions and guidance to help your child carry
the doll rapidly to the potty, rapidly lower her
pants, set the doll for a few seconds on the potty,
rapidly raise her pants, and carry her rapidly back to
where she "had the accident."

Emptying the pot into the toilet.

For each of the above steps, your child should tell the doll to practice; or, if he does not talk, ask him if she should practice—to which he should nod his head. Your child should give the doll three of these practice trials. Your child should then ask the doll if her pants are dry and guide the doll's hand to let the doll feel the wetness. Since the pants are wet, say, "No, Dolly, your pants are wet!"

Now have your child feel his own pants, and since they are dry, you praise him and give him a snack. Repeat the same procedure with the drink. Then

Flushing the toilet while holding on to the pot.

have your child assist the doll in changing her pants. Tell your child to show the doll where she should pee-pee by asking him to point to the potty chair. If your child does not know, instruct him and guide him to the potty chair, which he should touch. After about five minutes, indicate to the child that the doll is ready "to pee-pee like a big girl" and have the doll wet in the pot and praise her. As before, have your child empty the pot and have him make three more pants inspections spaced about five minutes apart. Thus, we end the imitation training period with the doll performing "like a big girl."

Putting the pot back in the chair.

How Long to Use the Doll

The doll demonstration trials should be given at the very start and should be continued until your child clearly understands the steps involved in toileting. No more than one hour is normally needed for this understanding. At the end of these demonstrations, your child will have learned how to dispose of the urine in the potty chair all by himself, what type of approval will result from correct toiletings, what type of disapproval for accidents, the need for sitting quietly on the potty chair, and all the other details of toileting oneself, all without necessarily having urinated even once himself.

Feeling the doll's dry pants and showing approval by giving her a snack treat.

Dry-Pants Inspections:
Creating the Motivation to Stay Dry

Inspect your child's pants for dryness every few minutes during the training period. These pants inspections will teach your child to be aware of his personal cleanliness and will give him the desire to remain clean and dry. You should call your child's attention to the condition of his pants and ask him if his pants are dry: "Are your pants dry?" Require him to feel the crotch area of his pants and then to indicate to you by word ("dry") or gesture (a head

Telling the doll that she shouldn't have wet her pants.

nod) that he is dry. Show your delight at his dry and clean pants by then giving him a drink or small treat, or both, and praising him for his dry pants. Initially, you should manually guide his hand to be sure that he is touching the correct part of his pants.

These inspections each require less than a minute and should be made about every three to five minutes whenever the child is not being given other instruction. A Training Reminder Sheet which contains spaces for recording the time of dry-pants inspections

70

Giving the doll practice in going to the potty.

can be found in Chapter 7, page 173. You should copy this sheet so that you have it at hand as a reminder to make the dry-pants inspections. During the Doll-That-Wets procedure, you should see to it that your child receives these dry-pants inspections at the same time that the doll receives hers.

Extra Drinks: Creating the Desire to Urinate

Give your child as much of the different beverages as he wants in order to create a strong and continuing desire to urinate. Start giving the drinks at the very beginning of training and even before that,

When you can feel that your pants are dry, you get a treat.

such as at the breakfast before you start training. Your child should continue to drink these extra drinks throughout training, ending only at the end of training. You should encourage him to drink at least eight ounces, which is one cup, every hour. Use different types of his favorite drink to create variety and to prevent him from tiring of one flavor or type of drink. Offer the drinks every few minutes, since your child probably will not drink a large volume at one time. To use the tasty drinks as a sign of your approval, give the drinks only as part of the approval you give him for having dry pants or for having toileted correctly. Do not give the drink without telling your child simultaneously what he has done that has pleased you, such as "Timmy has dry pants. Here is a drink for Timmy," or "Timmy sat on the potty. Timmy can have a drink."

Overcoming an Initial Reluctance to Drink

If your child is reluctant to drink the desired amount of fluids, several types of encouragement can be used. First, stimulate his thirst by including in your list of snack treats such salty items as peanuts, potato chips, pretzels, and corn chips. Second, use your child's natural tendency to imitate, by taking a small sip of the drink before you offer him the cup—or pretend to do so. Third, use the principle of "priming," by placing the cup against his lips and lifting it to the point at which he can taste the drink. Fourth, ensure that you have been offering his truly favorite drinks and in sufficient variety. Children will often indicate which drink they prefer if several types are placed before them.

Pants Raising and Lowering

During training you will have your child dressed in the loosely fitting pants, with a shirt if necessary for warmth, but without trousers or a dress. Younger children often experience some difficulty in dealing with their pants, especially in lowering them. One frequent problem is that their shirt hangs down in such a manner as to interfere with their grasp of the pants. To solve this problem, roll up the lower part of the shirt and pin it up, or better still, remove it entirely if the room temperature permits. Teaching your child to lower his pants is also facilitated

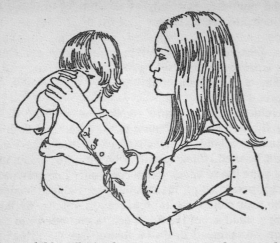

Your child will drink more if you make sure he actually tastes the drink.

by ensuring that the leg openings and waistband are sufficiently loose. In addition, have him bend his knees so that he will not have to bend over so far to lower his pants. When he is seated on the potty chair, have him position the pants below his knees where they will rest loosely and not bind him uncomfortably.

A problem encountered by young children with limited finger dexterity is that their protruding buttocks prevent them from sliding the pants up to their waist when dressing. To minimize this problem, teach your child to bend his knees slightly and to raise his pants by placing one hand behind his back, palm facing backward, when he grasps his pants by the waistband while grasping the front of the waistband with the other hand. This hand position causes the waistband to be lifted easily over the buttocks, especially as he straightens up from the bent-knee position.

Prompted Potty Trials:
Learning to Urinate in the Potty Chair

The major part of the instruction is given during the prompted potty trials during which you teach your child to perform each of the necessary pottying actions. You instruct your child to walk to the potty chair, to lower his pants, to seat himself on the chair, to sit quietly on the chair for several minutes, then to stand up again and to raise his pants. He is required to sit on the chair for several minutes at a time so that he will eventually urinate in that position and thereby learn through your resulting approval that he is expected to urinate there. When he has urinated in the potty chair, teach him to remove the pot, empty it into the household toilet, flush the toilet, and return the pot to the chair, where he reinserts it. These latter actions of emptying the pot will already have been taught to a large degree by the Doll-That-Wets procedure. An additional activity that you will teach during these trials is wiping oneself, which will be for girls after urination and bowel movements, but only after bowel movements for boys.

How Frequently He Practices Pottying

Give the prompted potty trials frequently, about fifteen minutes apart, at the start of training, and decrease their frequency as training progresses. As long as your child is having difficulty with any of the toileting skills, the trials should continue to be given frequently—about fifteen minutes apart. A Training Reminder Sheet which contains spaces for

A. Child dressed for training. Note loose-fitting training pants and pinned-up shirt.

B. Lowering pants: correct position of hands.

C. Raising pants (back view): correct position of hands.

D. Raising pants (side view): correct position of hands.

recording the time of prompted toiletings can be found in Chapter 7, page 174. You should copy this sheet so that you have it in front of you during the training. The two most common difficulties are lowering and raising the pants and/or reluctance to walk to the potty chair. Once the child is carrying out these actions without difficulty or reluctance, prompt him less and less frequently—about once every half hour or even more.

How Long to Sit on the Potty Chair

For the first few trials, you will have your child remain seated on the potty chair for a long period of time—about ten minutes. The purpose of his sitting on the potty for a long period is to ensure that when he does urinate he will do so in the potty and not in his pants. After he has urinated in the pot on two or three different trials, and been shown approval for doing so, he will realize that he should urinate in the pot. You will see that on repeated toileting trials he waits less and less time after seating himself before urinating. Once he has urinated in the pot, require him to be seated five minutes, but no more, on all of the following prompted trials. When your child walks to the toilet without being instructed to do so, let him determine how long he is to sit on the potty, since he will have sat down for the purpose of urinating and he will be the best judge of how much time he requires to initiate urination.

Eliminating the Need for Reminders to Potty Himself

Your child should learn to initiate the toileting sequence without being told to do so. To create this independence, you start with a direct instruction but

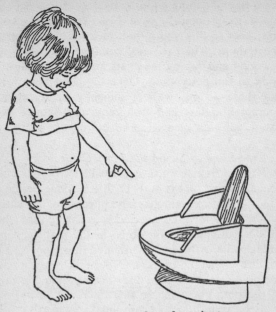

Child pointing to where he urinates.

then change to a question, then to a general statement about the potty, and finally merely comment
on his state of dryness. Use a direct instruction during the first two or three times you send him to the
potty ("Billy, go to the potty"). During the next few
trials, ask the general question as to whether he
desires to go ("Billy, do you want to potty?").
Next, make a general statement about the function
of the potty ("Billy, show me where you pee-pee").
Finally, make a general statement about his dry
pants ("Billy, are your pants dry?"), which is not a
reminder at all and is the standard question asked
as part of the dry-pants inspections.

When your child has walked to the potty chair after a direct instruction, use the general reminder on the very next trial and if necessary the next few trials until he reacts to the general reminder. Once he has gone to the potty chair after a general reminder, give the general statement about the potty on the very next trial or trials until he reacts by going to the chair. After that, you will only make a comment about his dry pants. If your child goes to the chair on the first trial when you made the comment, proceed to the next type of reminder on the very next trial. Once your child has advanced to the indirect reminders, do not give the more direct reminder on later trials. For example, if your child has proceeded to the potty chair when you asked him if he had to urinate, do not, at any later time, tell him to urinate in the potty chair.

When to Give the Prompting to Toilet

To increase the likelihood of urination after a prompting, try to give the prompting at a moment when your child has the desire to urinate. Some indications of this desire are that your child will hold his genitals, cross his legs together, suddenly change to a somber expression, walk with his thighs close together, or start pacing. If you had intended to give a prompted toileting trial in a few minutes, give the prompting earlier and as soon as you observe this type of "body signal" that he desires to urinate.

Relaxation Needed Before Urinating

Another factor that determines whether your child urinates on a given trial is his state of relaxation as he is seated on the potty. If your child is shifting about on the seat, attempting to stand up, or is mentally preoccupied—say, with television, or a visitor or a toy or conversation—he is not likely to urinate, since urination is more likely in a state of mental and physical relaxation.

How to Ensure Relaxation
While the Child Is Sitting on the Potty

To ensure this relaxed state, praise and reassure your child. If he is moving about while seated, give praise at those moments when he is even briefly relaxed: "That's good: Billy is sitting quietly; Billy is quiet" and use gentle manual guidance to restrain any restless body or hand movements. Once your child has become less restless, decrease the manual guidance and decrease the praise, since the manual contact or conversation will be distracting and prevent the desired state of quiet relaxation. Very infrequently, remind your child of your concern by praising his relaxation with a brief statement of approval for his maintained state relaxation ("Billy sits just like his daddy"). If he is very restless or reluctant to sit on the chair on the first trial, require him to remain seated for only a minute or two, praising him whenever he begins to relax and allowing him to arise as soon as a few seconds of relaxation have occurred. On the next trial, you will be able to require him to stay seated for a few minutes longer.

Immediate Detection of Urinations in the Potty

To emphasize the importance of urinating in the pot, your child should be praised as soon as he starts to urinate there. Therefore, you should take

several steps to ensure that you will detect urination
as soon as it starts. The best method is to teach
your child to tell you when he is urinating. Do this
at the time that he first sits on the potty: "Betty,
pee-pee in the potty. Tell me when you pee-pee.
What will you say when you pee-pee?" or "Point
to the potty when you pee-pee. Where will you
point when you pee-pee?" As was stated previously,
conversation with your child must be discontinued
once he is sitting quietly. Consequently, give him
these instructions only when he first sits down and
while he is not yet relaxed. Since your child may
not always tell you when he is urinating, you should
watch the pot closely so that you will detect the
urination yourself. Several techniques are helpful
in providing immediate detection: 1) Look continuously between your child's legs for signs of
urine in the pot. 2) Have the pants lowered well below the knees, so that they will allow the knees to
be spread apart. 3) Teach your child to keep his
knees apart and to keep his hands on his legs rather
than on his lap. 4) Arrange the chair in such a way
that the overhead illumination does not cast a
shadow on the pot opening. 5) Place a large piece
of absorbent tissue, such as a napkin or facial or
toilet tissue, on the bottom of the pot. The darkening
of the paper when it is wet will be more conspicuous,
especially if the tissue is colored. 6) Kneel in front
of the pot for better visibility, if necessary. 7) Teach
your child to sit well back in the chair so that more
of the pot will be visible. 8) If your closeness to the
child distracts him, stand at a distance with your
head oriented slightly away from him but your eyes
still on the pot.

Posture While Seated

If a boy is seated improperly on the potty chair, his stream of urine may miss the potty. If this problem exists, teach him to lean slightly forward while he is seated.

Genital Exploration

It is not uncommon for young children, especially little boys, to touch their genitals while sitting on the potty. This activity creates the problem that your child may become too preoccupied to concentrate on urinating. You can easily discourage this fondling by distracting him. Matter-of-factly call your child by name, offer him a favorite toy to hold, or simply talk to him. Do not criticize or punish him. Once your child is even partially trained, the problem will disappear, since he will be spending very little time on the potty.

Creating the Motivation for Correct Toileting by Approval

Enthusiasm

Your child's motivation to toilet himself correctly will depend on the manner in which you give him approval. Use all of the five major types of approval at your disposal: 1) verbal praise, 2) snack treats, 3) the drinks, 4) the Friends-Who-Care procedure (see pages 87-88), and 5) the nonverbal praise of hugging, stroking, smiling, and even clapping. These acts of approval must be very desirable to your child, so that he will be motivated by them. Accordingly, give these motivators in a way that shows your extreme pleasure and that delights him. Be enthusiastic, exuberant, excited, expressive, and let this

You did it right! You did it!

delight be very visible. Your silent pleasure cannot be expected to motivate your child. A good guideline is to overreact: praise loudly, smile very broadly, hug him close, clap your hands, state your praise in several ways, and kiss him. When you see that your child is vibrating with excited joy, you will know that your expressive display of pleasure has been adequately communicated.

Approval for Doing Well:
Explain Why You Are Pleased
If your child is to be motivated by your approval to toilet correctly, he must understand why you are

Receiving candy for a job well done.

giving him the approval. Consequently, whenever you praise him, always tell him why you are praising him. Never give approval without letting him understand what it was he did that has caused you to show your approval. For example, when you applaud and hug him when he urinates in the potty, tell him "Billy peed in the potty, I'm so happy"; or when he is sitting on the potty chair, "Billy is sitting so quiet" as you rub his back; or when he pulls his pants down, "Billy is like a big boy. He is pulling his

A hug to show you appreciate his efforts to please you.

pants down"; or simply for being dry, "Here's candy for Billy. Billy has dry pants."

When to Use a Specific Type of Motivator

Use all of the types of motivators throughout training, but be guided in the choice of motivators by the degree to which the motivator interrupts your child. The snack treat, the drink, the hug, and the stroke all require you to interrupt your child in what he is doing. Consequently, give these types of approval only at those times when the use of the motivator will not interfere with the toileting sequence, such as at the dry-pants inspection, after he has urinated in the potty, and after he has replaced the pot in the chair. You can use all the other motivators for all actions without concern for interruption, since these other motivators are primarily verbal and do not entail body contact.

Think Positive

At the start of training, the approval should be almost continuous, to establish a warm, positive atmosphere and to encourage every correct action. In order to give approval only for specific actions and yet to give approval continuously, you must "think positive." Do not think about what the child cannot do, but about what he or she can do. Even at the start of training, when the child has not learned very much, praise those few actions he or she *has* learned—for example, "Sarah has pants on. She is like a big girl," or "Sarah sat on the potty. Sarah sits so nicely," or "Sarah has dry pants," etc.

Approval at the Start of an Action

When teaching a new action, do not wait for the action to be completed before showing approval. Rather, show approval at the very start of the action. For example, when your child starts to walk to the chair on the first toileting trial, praise him when he starts to take his first step ("Johnny is walking to the potty; Johnny is a big boy"). Continue to show approval as he continues the action, such as when he reaches the chair ("Look at Johnny at the potty. Won't Daddy be happy!"). Similarly, when he first touches his pants to lower them, while he is lowering them, and as he backs into the chair, praise and applaud him. When he sits down, praise him as he sits quietly. Praise him at the very start of urination. Give the snack treat, drink, praise, applause, and hug after his urination has stopped, etc. Even if some manual guidance and direct instructions were needed to obtain the actions, give your child approval for each of these steps as he assists in carrying out the actions. By praising him for each small action, you will be motivating him to attempt the next step, in the justified expectation that he will receive continued approval, and you will be motivating him to do it by himself during the next trial.

Approval at the End of an Action

As you observe that your child is performing the actions correctly and willingly, give the approval at the completion of an action rather than continuously during the action—such as when he reaches the chair rather than as he walks to the chair, and after he has replaced the potty after emptying it rather than continuously while he was emptying and replacing it. Then delay the approval still further, so that you wait until several actions are completed before showing approval. When the child is enthusiastically and correctly performing the entire toileting sequence, the approval should be given only for the last step—namely, the replacement of the emptied potty in the chair.

Termination of Approval for Toileting

Once your child has required only the approval for replacing the potty, give no further approval for the toiletings, either during or after. You wish to teach him to remain clean and dry. Accordingly, reserve your approval for his having dry pants, which is what is done at the dry-pants inspections, thereby motivating your child to be dry and not simply to toilet himself. Otherwise, he might continue to seek your approval indefinitely for toileting.

Friends-Who-Care Procedure

Your child's new attitude toward cleanliness will be formed more rapidly if you convey to him that all of his friends are as concerned about his cleanliness as you are. To communicate this shared concern by others, when you give approval tell your child how delighted his close friends are with him also. Use the list of people on the Friends-Who-Care list you have prepared. When you give approval for an action, continually give the approval in the name of one of those persons—such as "Tommy is sitting on the potty; Grandmother will be so happy," or "Eddie [his brother] will say, 'Tommy is a big boy.'" Also describe the similarity between your child's approved actions and those of the close friends—for example, "Good boy, Tommy. You flushed the toilet. Just like Daddy." Or "Your pants are dry. Just like Captain Kangaroo's." Rotate the use of names in such a way that you name all persons on the Friends-Who-Care list several times. Whenever possible, describe the anticipated approval of a friend in a manner that actually can be carried out soon. For example, "When Daddy comes home today, he'll say, 'Tommy is a big boy. Tommy has dry pants.'" Or "When Eddie sees you go potty, he'll be so happy"; or "Grandma will be so happy when we call her." Then as soon as training is completed that day, have Grandma tell him of her pleasure over the phone, and have his father and brother do likewise when they arrive home.

Creating Understanding Through Verbal Rehearsal

Your child has a great capacity for understanding. Once he understands what is expected, he will have less difficulty learning his new attitude about cleanliness. The two things you wish to have your child understand are 1) that he should toilet in the potty and 2) that he should not wet his pants.

The verbal rehearsal procedure teaches your child this understanding by telling him what the correct toileting actions are, what benefits will result from correct toileting, and what benefits he would miss by not learning correct toileting. For example, say, "Mommy will be happy when you pee-pee in the potty. Will you pee-pee in the potty?" (He nods his head indicating "Yes.") "Will you pee-pee in your pants?" (He shakes his head, indicating "No.") "Where will you pee-pee? Show me." (He points to the potty.) "Will you get crackers if you pee-pee in the potty? (He nods.) "Will you get crackers if you pee-pee in your pants?" (Shakes his head, "No.") "Does Daddy pee-pee in his pants?" ("No.") "Do big boys pee-pee in their pants?" ("No.") "You will go potty by yourself. Will you potty by yourself?" ("Yes.") "Daddy potties by himself. Does Mommy potty by herself?" ("Yes.")

This same rehearsal should be used for any part of training that is causing a problem. For example, if your child is reluctant to wear pants and wants his diapers, describe the desirability of pants and undesirability of diapers with statements such as "Babies wear diapers. Does Daddy wear diapers?" ("No.") "Big boys wear pants. Does Eddie wear pants?" ("Yes.") "Are you a big boy like Eddie?" ("Yes.") This verbal rehearsal should be given continually. As is indicated in the above examples, give approval in the name of persons from the Friends-Who-Care list when you show your approval. This constant verbal rehearsal enables you to teach your child all the future advantages of personal cleanliness with-

When giving instructions, always make sure that your child is looking at you and that he answers you by word or gesture—for example, an affirmative head nod.

out having to wait for him to experience those advantages.

Attention

To ensure that you gain your child's attention, call him by name before speaking to him. Also, whenever you give him information, ensure that the child understands your information by having him answer a simple question about what you have told him. As is illustrated in the previous examples, have your child answer either by gesturing, by nodding his head, or by speaking, if he can. When your child answers correctly, give him immediate approval for doing so, such as "That's right, Billy," and hug him or give him a drink. If he does not answer correctly, tell him what the correct answer is and ask the question again. "Billy, does Daddy wear diapers?" . . . "No. Daddy doesn't wear diapers. Billy, does Daddy wear diapers?" Do not give additional information and do not ask another question until he has correctly answered the present one. If he does not seem to be paying attention or listening and does not answer, orient his head toward you until he is looking steadily at your face, call him again by name, and then repeat the question.

Instructions

The principal method of teaching your child what to do is to use verbal instructions. For these instructions to be effective, you should give them in a manner that is suited to your child's limited language ability. Here are several rules to follow in giving your child instructions.

Call Him by Name

Before starting an instruction after a silent period, say your child's name, so that he will know you are speaking to him. Say, "Marty, go to the potty"— not "Go to the potty," or "Go to the potty, Marty."

Stand Close

Also, before starting an instruction, do not stand at a distance from your child while you are telling him what to do. Instead, stand within easy arm's reach before you start speaking. This closeness will enable you to guide him manually if he does not know what you wish him to do.

Point

Whenever possible, point or gesture during the instruction as a further aid to his understanding. Point to the doll, or his pants, or the potty, or the toilet flush handle, or whatever object you are telling him about.

Be Brief

Make each instruction brief so that he can understand you more easily. For example, do not say "Now, Marty, what I want you to do is to try to lift up the potty bowl that is in the middle of the chair that you have been using." More easily understood is the brief instruction, "Marty, pick up the potty bowl," while you point at the bowl.

Use the Same Words

Use the same wording each time. Do not say "Marty, feel your pants" at one time and "Marty, touch yourself" at another time. These slight word changes can be confusing.

Guiding the child's hands.

Be Detailed at First

Make the instructions very specific at the start of training, and as your child learns to carry out the actions, make the instructions more general. For example, at the start of training the instruction "Marty, pull up your pants" may be too global to a child unfamiliar with dressing. If your child looks at all

93

confused, be more specific and say, "Marty, bend over," then "Grab your pants, Now, grab with this hand. Grab with that hand. Yes, grab with both hands. Now, pull up, up, up. Pull the pants to your tummy." Because of this need for details at the start of training, you should expect to give the verbal instructions almost continuously at that time, just as you give almost continuous approval at that time. On successive trials, make the instructions more general again, so that as your child learns, you will be giving as little instruction as possible.

Be Enthusiastic

Your tone of voice while giving an instruction should exhibit warmth and optimism that your child will obey, and never indicate impatience or irritability. To help convey this optimism, show your child approval as he carries out each of your instructions, such as "Marty, bend over. That's good! Grab your pants. Yes, that's right, with your hand. Now, grab with this hand. Wonderful! You're holding it just right! Now, grab with both hands. Beautiful! You're doing so well! Now, pull up, up, up. Yes, you're almost done. Now pull the pants up to your tummy. You did it! Just like Daddy. You pulled up your pants; just like Daddy does!"

Manual Guidance: Ensuring That an Action Will Be Carried Out

Whenever your child does not carry out your instructions—either because he does not completely understand the instructions or because he is reluctant—gently but firmly guide your child's hands, legs, or body through the proper motions. The guidance should be as slight as possible. Consequently, grasp

94

your child as lightly as possible while still maintaining sufficient firmness to guide him. Be very sensitive to his actions; when you feel him trying to complete the action, immediately lighten your grasp to a mere touch, thereby allowing him to complete the movement himself. Further reduce the guidance by removing your hand entirely as he continues the action, but keep your hands near him so that you can again grasp him and begin guiding should his actions falter or be misdirected.

Use Manual Guidance After Instructions

As was stated previously, when you first give your child an instruction, you should be within easy arm's reach of the child while you give the instruction. Wait about a second after giving the instruction to see if your child is following the instruction. If he starts to follow your instruction within that brief waiting period, do not manually guide him, but rather observe him closely and remain near him so that you can begin guiding if he becomes confused or stops his motion. If he does not begin to move correctly during that one- or two-second period after the instruction, lightly touch him for a moment; then gently guide him if the mere touch does not remind him effectively of the need for action.

Types of Actions to Be Guided

If any instruction you give for an action is not followed immediately, the action should be guided. Guide by grasping the child's shoulders when you have given instructions to go to the potty chair, to sit on and arise from the chair, and to take the pot to and from the toilet. Guide his hands or fingers by grasping them in your hands when guiding his pants raising, wiping, removing and reinserting the pot in the chair, emptying the pot, flushing the toilet, and having him feel his pants during the dry-pants inspections. Guide his legs when he is dressing in clean pants after an accident.

How Much Guidance to Use and When

Manual guidance will be needed more at the start of training than later, since your child will have learned by then how to carry out the actions. As you see that your child is responding to the instruction with no need for manual guidance, you should begin standing farther away from him during the instruction, so that he can learn to be independent. For this same reason of avoiding overdependence on your help, you should not manually guide your child if he is making some attempt to perform the action. The guidance should always be as gentle and mild as possible while still ensuring that the action is completed.

Reluctance to Follow Instructions

Manual guidance will also be needed more at those moments when your child is reluctant to carry out your instructions. Such instances may occur at any point, depending on a child's sudden change of mood. Generally speaking, manual guidance is needed more often when previous training experiences have been unpleasant or unsuccessful than when there has been no previous attempt at training. You should also expect a greater need for manual guidance after an accident, since many children are somewhat reluctant initially to carry out the corrective actions and practice trials that are required after an accident. When your child shows reluctance to follow an instruction, do not allow this reluctance to dissuade you from manually guiding him through the instructed action.

Let Me Do It Myself, Mommy

When your child delays in carrying out your instruction, you will probably have a very strong temptation to carry out the action yourself rather than wait for him to do it in the slow, uncertain manner that will characterize his early efforts. For example, you tell him, "Jimmy, pull your pants down," and he awkwardly tries to grasp the waistband and cannot lower the pants with the one hand he is using. Or you say, "Johnny, pick up the potty bowl," and he fumbles for several seconds trying to remove the bowl from the potty chair. You will have a strong tendency to grasp the pants yourself and pull them down or to put your own fingers under the edge of the potty bowl and pick it up for him. Although you will accomplish the action much faster than he can, he will not have learned how to do it himself. The solution to this problem is to guide both hands through the necessary motions by the gentle-guidance procedure. In that manner, the action will be carried out fairly quickly but he will not become dependent on your doing it for him. You have helped him to help himself. Resist this urge to do it for him by substituting instead the more instructive procedure of guiding him.

Accidents (Pants Wetting)

What to Do When He Wets His Pants

The instruction gives your child the attitude that he should never wet his pants. Nevertheless, one or more accidents may occur. When an accident does occur, you will carry out four procedures. First, show visible disapproval to demonstrate your displeasure at wet pants. Second, require your child to practice the toileting actions that would have prevented the accident by using a procedure designated as Positive Practice. Third, make him aware of the wetness of his pants and of the social disapproval that results from wet pants. Fourth, teach your child to assume responsibility for his pants wetting by requiring him to change into dry pants himself. We will now describe these four steps in more detail.

Verbal Disapproval for Pants Wetting

As soon as you see that your child has wet his pants, reprimand him immediately and with sufficient emphasis to make him realize that pants wetting is not a grown-up action. Try especially to show your disapproval immediately after the wetting by loudly saying "No!" as soon as you detect the wetting, in the hope that your loud voice will cause the urination to be interrupted. Then tell him why you are displeased by statements such as "You wet your pants" or "Your pants are wet." Express your disappointment by pointing out that you are not pleased with what he has done. "Wetting is bad," or "Big boys don't like wet pants," or "Mommy doesn't like wet pants," or "Only babies like wet pants." These reprimands should be given only for the first few seconds after the pants wetting has been detected. Children vary greatly in their reaction to disapproval. For most children, simple verbal disapproval may be sufficient. Other children may require more emphatic disapproval, but spanking or other physical punishment is probably never necessary or justified.

Positive Practice of Self-Toileting
After an Accident

After you have given your child the immediate reprimand for pants wetting, require him to practice the act of walking rapidly to the potty chair and preparing to toilet himself. You wish him to learn by this intensive practice to rapidly toilet himself so that he will learn how to go quickly to the potty chair the next time that he has the need to urinate. Tell him what you are doing and why. "Billy wet his pants. Billy has to practice going to the potty." Guide him to the location where his wetting occurred and tell him "Practice going to potty. Practice quickly." Require him to walk rapidly to the potty chair, to lower his pants, and to sit on the potty—but only for one second. Do not allow time for urination to occur in the potty, and do not encourage him to try to urinate. He has already released some of his urine in his pants and probably does not have an irresistible desire to urinate further at this time. More important, you wish your child to learn to urinate in the potty on his own. So, within a second or two after he has sat down, have him arise. Then have him raise his pants quickly and walk quickly to another location in the room, where you immediately start another Positive Practice trial without delay. Have him carry out ten of these trials. About two of these trials should be started from the location where he had the accident, so that he will be reenacting the wetting situation but this time taking positive action. The other eight trials should be started from very remote

Positive Practice after an accident:
A. Mother guiding child to practice walking rapidly to the potty.

locations in the room, and from other rooms, so that he will learn to go to the potty from any place in the house.

Require your child to move very rapidly in walking to and from the potty chair as well as in lowering and raising his pants. Instruct him as to what he is to do and why he must do it (he wet his pants), and remind him of the need for speed. "Billy wet his pants. Billy must practice. Practice going to the potty chair. Practice quickly. Practice pulling

B. Guiding child's hands in lowering his wet pants rapidly.

your pants down. Practice quickly. You wet your pants. Practice Sitting. Practice quickly. Practice getting up—quickly; you wet your pants. Practice pulling your pants up; practice quickly. Now practice going from the bedroom. Practice quickly going to the bedroom." If he does not move quickly as you have instructed, manually guide him rapidly through the desired action. These Positive Practice trials will ensure that he knows how to go to the toilet from different locations and to do so rapidly

Wet pants are no fun.

should there be an urgent need to urinate in the future.

Wet-Pants Awareness After an Accident

After the Positive Practice trials, the third step is to make your child aware of his wet pants. Provide at least ten pants inspections, the first of them immediately after the last Positive Practice period. Ask your child if he has dry pants and have him feel his pants. Since he is still wearing his wet pants, he will feel the wetness. Then tell him how unhappy you and his heroes are that his pants are wet. Then tell him again to feel his pants and again tell him how you and his friends do not like wet pants, continuing in this manner for ten wet-pants inspections. This procedure will make him very aware of the difference between wet and dry pants by requiring

102

him to feel the wet pants and will teach him that you, his friends, and his heroes all do not like wet pants. You should record the wet-pants inspections on the Training Reminder Sheet; see page 173.

Cleanliness Responsibility for a Pants Wetting

The fourth and last procedure you follow after an accident is the Cleanliness Responsibility procedure, which educates your child to assume responsibility for remedying his untidiness. After the last wet-pants inspection, require him to change into clean, dry pants. Do not change the pants for him. You may, however, have to manually guide his legs into the pants legs, especially if he has not yet learned to dress. Using minimum manual assistance, require him to remove his wet pants. Have him carry the wet pants to the usual location of the soiled-clothes hamper, into which he places them. Have him obtain the dry pants from an accessible location where you have placed them. Have him put them on. If any urine has caused a noticeable wetness on the floor, have him obtain a sponge or cloth from an accessible location and have him wipe up the wetness. This wiping should be done immediately after the wetting to avoid a permanent stain. By having him change himself and clean up himself, you will be educating him as to why you are concerned about pants wetting and educating him to correct any accidents in the future.

These four steps teach your child 1) that disapproval will be given for wet pants, 2) how to toilet rapidly to avoid wetting his pants, 3) the difference between wet and dry pants, and finally, 4) how to correct the state of untidiness that resulted from the pants wetting. If your child wets

Cleanliness Responsibility Training after an accident:
A. Taking off his wet pants by himself.
B. Carrying wet pants to the dirty-clothes hamper.

his pants during the first few minutes of training before he has learned how to toilet himself at all, do not give all four steps. Simply give the immediate verbal disapproval and the Cleanliness Responsibility procedure. Once he has completed one of the prompted toileting trials, however, he knows the correct manner of toileting; all four steps should be followed for any pants wetting thereafter. If these four corrective steps are followed after a pants wetting, very few "accidents" should occur.

Love Your Child, but Disapprove of Wetting

Do not become angry with your child when he has an accident. Do not show anger in your voice or actions when you carry out the four corrective steps for wetting. Your attitude should be that you love your child as much as ever, even though you dislike wet pants. You will, therefore, react to his accident by giving him constructive instruction rather than inflicting pain. To ensure this positive outlook, keep your tone of voice at an even level and do not shout (except for the initial statement of "No" when you first detect wetting). Do not slap or spank him, since these actions only cause distress without teaching him how to prevent or correct accidents in the future and without teaching him why you are so distressed.

As you require your child to carry out the Positive Practice trials, the Wet-Pants-Awareness procedure, and the Cleanliness Responsibility procedure, provide explanations of each of the actions you take. So, for example, say, "You didn't potty fast; you wet your pants. Go to the potty; go fast," and "Your pants are wet; take off your pants," and continually say "Practice" to explain why he must go repeatedly to the potty. You continuously explain that your dislike of wet pants is shared by others whom he wishes to emulate. He will certainly dislike having to change his pants and to practice pottying in a rapid manner, but he will understand why this instruction and correction are necessary. When your child wets his pants, look upon him as requiring intensive practice in how to prevent and correct it and not as an object of punishment.

Tantrums

For most children, the training is a pleasant experience, filled with continuous adult praise and warmth, and the child cooperates eagerly. However, some children will tantrum, especially at the very start of training. Of course, if the child has a history of throwing tantrums, he is also more likely to do so during toilet training, whereas a child who has not had frequent tantrums before training probably will not have them during training. A child who has previously received unsuccessful or harsh toilet training is more likely to resist another attempt. Children who have not been trained previously will rarely resist on this first attempt.

If your child shows resistance or has a tantrum, do not allow that resistance to interrupt the instruction. Follow the required sequence of instructing him and guiding him when necessary and then showing approval for his correct actions when the resistance is absent or even reduced. He will realize that you will not allow his tantrum or "fussing" to postpone his performance of the action and that your profuse praise results when he cooperates.

You are teaching the child one small skill at a time with repeated detailed instructions, demonstrations, mental rehearsal, and praise. He will learn after his first tantrum that you are not requiring him to do more than he is capable of doing easily, but that you do expect him to do as you say. Even for children who are very prone to tantrum, you should not experience more than two or three incidents in which he is "testing" your intentions.

What Happens If the Child Is Not Trained in One Day?

As was stated previously, the average child requires about one-half day to be trained by the present procedure. For a small proportion of children, training will not be completed within one day. If this should happen with your child, leave him in his training pants at the end of that first day's training. Continue periodically, during the remainder of that day and evening, to remind him that he should keep himself dry by using the potty and that he should not wet his pants. Under no circumstances should he be dressed back in diapers or taken to the potty. If he has an accident, follow the usual procedure for accidents. Begin training the following day at the same point at which the training had ended the previous day. For example, if he was going to the potty in response to your general suggestions at the end of the day, you would not revert back to giving him direct instructions the next day.

Termination of Training

You may consider your child to be trained when he walks to the potty chair for the first time without a reminder and completes the entire toileting experience without the need for instructions or guidance. Nevertheless, you should continue to observe him potty a few more times so that you can fade out the inspections and approval for toileting. Watch him initiate about three more completely independent toiletings, but do not give any approval after the third of these self-toiletings. The snack treats and approval should be given only at the pants inspections, which should be made less and less frequently—about every ten to fifteen minutes. During the time between pants inspections, continue to conduct the verbal rehearsal procedure in which you describe to him the desirability of his keeping his pants dry. You should now be making him realize that he has completely mastered a grown-up skill, that he should be openly proud of his mastery, and that you and all of his important friends will share his pride. After the first completely independent toileting, start introducing some of his toys or games, so that he can learn to interrupt these games to toilet himself. Continue giving him the fluids to maintain the desire to urinate, and be alert for pants wetting until he has initiated toileting himself several times and has had no accidents.

After he has toileted himself several times, you can put away all the training materials and supplies. Allow him to watch television or play by himself with the potty chair nearby. You are now free to resume your other activities. For the remainder of the day, check his pants every hour or so, especially when other family members return home. The next day, begin checking his pants according to the After Training schedule described in Chapter 5.

CHAPTER 5

After Training

At this stage, your child has spent a few hours learning to toilet in the potty chair after having spent several years wetting his diapers or pants. Small wonder that a child might conclude that the brief training period was just a game and that pants wetting will be permitted the next day. The purpose of the After Training procedure is to teach your child that your concern about his toileting is permanent.

Pants Inspections After Training

For several days after training, continue to conduct pants inspections—especially during the first day or two, when your child understandably will be testing your changed attitude. Conduct a pants inspection before each meal, before between-meal snacks, before nap times, and before bedtime, providing about six or seven inspections each day. These events have been selected as inspection times because they are events that almost all children experience every day. If other events occur regularly in your family schedule—such as when a brother or sister returns from school at midafternoon, when you return from some activity, or when the father returns from work in the late afternoon —consider adding an inspection at those times.

Happiness is dry pants.

Conduct the inspection just as you did during training: by asking your child whether his pants are dry and requiring him to touch his pants. If they are dry, praise him enthusiastically. Do not use the snack treat or drink after training; they are not necessary now. Show your approval by praising him. Whenever possible, have some other family member or visitor conduct the inspection, such as the father, brother, sister, aunt, grandparent, etc. We suggest you make a copy of, and use, the After Training Reminder Sheet (see page 175) to remind yourself when to conduct the pants inspections.

Accidents After Training

You should expect your child to have a small number of accidents during the first few days after training. He will be learning to use his new skills under different situations and conditions of distraction. You, in turn, must not allow any accident to go uncorrected, or all the training benefits will disappear and he will continue to wet his pants. If his pants are found wet at the inspection, or at any other time, reprimand him. Then, after you have required the usual ten Positive Practice trials, require him to change into dry pants himself. Omit only the Wet-Pants-Awareness procedure at this time—since he is undoubtedly now aware of the difference between wet and dry pants. You should give this corrective action whenever you find that his pants are wet, but most detections of wet pants are likely to occur at the time of one of the regularly scheduled dry-pants inspections. These inspections are scheduled right before mealtimes, snack times, nap times, and bedtime. Consequently, be sure that he practices toileting and changes himself first. Then allow

111

him to have the snack or meal or nap or whatever other activity was scheduled. After he has remained dry for about one week, you may discontinue the practice trials, but continue to give the reprimand and to expect him to change himself.

Terminating the Pants Inspections

When your child has gone one week without having an accident, discontinue the scheduled pants-inspection periods. Do not hesitate to comment spontaneously, however, on his toileting skills or his dry clothing whenever an opportunity presents itself.

Trips

Your child will require that a potty chair be available until he is tall enough to use an adult toilet by himself. Whenever you go on a trip or visit away from home, take the potty chair with you, or teach your child to ask for assistance in using an adult-sized toilet. On a short trip of less than an hour or so, ask your child whether he wants to go to the potty before you leave.

Outdoor Accidents

Your child is more likely to have an accident outdoors than in the house. Some of the reasons for this difference are that he may be very much preoccupied in the outdoor activity, that the access to the potty in his home is difficult (the outside doors may be hard for him to open), and that he may be dressed in heavy outdoor clothing that is difficult to remove. You can reduce these outdoor accidents by asking him whether he wishes to potty before leaving the house, by ensuring easy entrance into the

By virtue of the authority vested in her
as potty trainer,

_____

Trainer's name

has conferred on

_____

Child's name

_____

Child's age

The degree of P.T. (Potty-Trained)
and has granted this Diploma
as evidence this   day of   , 19

day   *month*   *year*

Thereof

Mother   *Father*

A big achievement deserves a diploma.

house, and by using only outdoor clothing that he has learned to remove. When you provide the Positive Practice trials for any such outdoor accidents, the trials should be given from the outdoor location where the accident occurred; you will thus have an opportunity to discover what aspect of the novel outdoor situation may have caused the problem.

Bowel Movements

No separate training is needed for bowel movements. Since defecation does not usually occur without urination, the training for urination will usually generalize to defecation. An ironic problem that sometimes arises in training is that the training for correct urination is usually completed so rapidly that your child may not have defecated even once during training and therefore could not be given the approval for having done so. Bowel training may have to occur after the training for urination, but you can accomplish it simply by treating a bowel accident in the exact same manner as a wetting accident: reprimand him for soiling himself, give him the ten Positive Practice trials in toileting himself, and require him to change his soiled clothing himself. Bowel control normally occurs at an earlier age than does urinary control and seems to be a much easier skill for most children to learn. Consequently, once you have trained your child to urinate properly, he should have no problem with his bowel movements.

Diapers

You have now taught your child to toilet himself. Should he ever wear diapers again—and if so, under what circumstances?

Your child should never again wear diapers during the day. But what if he has a physical condition, such as a bad case of diarrhea, that makes wetting or bowel movements difficult to avoid? If so, use plastic pants over his training pants instead of putting him back in diapers. The reason for using pants is that you do not wish to prevent him from toileting himself if he still has some control. Diapers are so difficult for a child to remove that he would then lose his motivation to even try. Diapers should be worn during the day only when illness confines your child to his bed.

Nighttime is a different story. If your child is younger than about 2½ years of age, continue to dress the child in diapers at bedtime. If your child is older than about 2½ years, dress him in training pants. To protect your mattress, place a plastic or rubber sheet under the top bed sheet. The diapers are then eliminated completely for the older child, and will not prevent him from toileting himself if he awakens during the night. Some children will begin staying dry at night simply as a result of the daytime training.

Diploma

The Diploma on the next page should be filled in when your child has completed his potty training, thereby providing you with a permanent record of your joint achievement.

CHAPTER 6

Mrs. James Potty-Trains Mickey

The following account describes the thoughts and actions of a mother while training her son with the new training method. The names are fictitious, and the circumstances, actions, and outcomes are a composite of the typical events that have occurred during training.

Mrs. Lee James decided that it was time to potty-train her youngest child, Mickey, who would be 2 years of age in a few weeks. The very thought of training him made her apprehensive. She realized that the training had to be done and yet dreaded having to do it.

Her oldest child, Ronnie, aged 8, had not been completely trained until he was 37 months old. She had started training Ronnie at 18 months in what became over a year and a half of frustration for both of them. Ronnie had resisted at every step along the way: he cried whenever he was placed on the potty; he would hide whenever he had a B.M.; he acted lazy and uncooperative; he refused to wear training pants, requesting instead that she dress him in diapers. Ronnie finally became trained when his younger cousin, Todd, came for a visit. Todd was three months younger than Ronnie but had been potty-trained for several months. Ronnie accompanied Todd to the toilet a few times and began spontaneously using the toilet thereafter.

Four-year-old Renée, the Jameses' middle child, had been potty-trained at 2½. Mrs. James had begun Renée's training when she turned 2. Although Renée did not display Ronnie's defiant attitude toward training, it took Mrs. James six months of rigid adherence to a regular schedule of placing Renée on the potty several times a day before her training was completed.

Mrs. James wasn't sure how Mickey would react to training. Since he was a boy, he might act like Ronnie or he might be somewhat easier to train, as Renée was; but even then, several months would still be required to complete the training.

Mrs. James was determined to find a better way of toilet training that would produce less wear and tear on her and Mickey. She had heard about a training method that told how to train the average 24-month-old child to potty himself in less than a day. Although this claim sounded impossible, Mrs. James decided to give the training method a try. After she had familiarized herself with the program, she felt ready to begin.

The first step was to find out if Mickey was ready to be potty-trained. Mrs. James determined his readiness by giving him three tests. She wanted to know if he had 1) some control of his bladder muscles, 2) sufficient physical coordination, and 3) sufficient understanding and willingness to follow instructions. Mickey passed the Bladder Readiness Test easily. Two factors had convinced her that Mickey had at least partial and perhaps complete bladder control. First, he would often remain dry for three or four hours at a time. Second, he would often clutch himself a minute or two before urinating, indicating that he could feel that his bladder was full. Mickey also passed the Physical Readiness Test. She knew he had the necessary physical coordination: he walked well, with excellent balance, and was quite adept with his fingers. In fact, she often wished that he were not quite so agile; he always seemed to be exploring everything, thereby requiring her to keep a constant eye on him. The results of the third test, however —the one for Instructional Readiness—were very disappointing.

Throughout the Instructional Readiness Test, Mickey balked at following the instructions, even though he had performed the requested actions on many previous occasions. He had refused to follow at least half of the ten instructions she had given him. It became very clear to her, right then, that Mickey's stubbornness must be overcome before she could give any further serious thought to potty-training him. She would postpone his training until he could be taught to follow instructions reliably. Fortunately, in reading a description of the training procedure, she had picked up some helpful hints on how to overcome Mickey's obstinacy. In general, she tried to be enthusiastic when he did follow instructions, to stand nearby whenever she instructed him, to guide him manually if he did not react to an instruction, to give instructions only when Mickey was looking at her, and not to allow him to tantrum as a means of avoiding having to follow the instruction.

After two weeks, she was delighted by the fruits of her labors. Mickey had become a very responsive child who seemed to delight in the pleasure he now gave his mother. Mickey's metamorphosis from stubbornness to a willingness to please convinced Mrs. James that he was ready for training. But first she would give Mickey the Instructional Readiness Test again. This time he passed the test with ease.

In addition to having taught Mickey to follow instructions during the preceding few weeks, Mrs. James had arranged for him to have some other experiences that she felt would also help him during the training. She had begun asking him to do as much of his dressing as he could. Naturally, she had concentrated on teaching him to lower and raise his pants. She had used the same loose-fitting training pants that she intended to use during his potty training. She concentrated on teaching him the phrases "pull up" and "pull down." She asked all of the family members to have Mickey accompany them to the toilet so that he could watch and learn what they were doing. She asked them to explain each step to Mickey—such as "Mickey, look, I'm pulling up my pants." They had even let Mickey flush the toilet for them. During these trips to the toilet and at other times, Mrs. James had been making sure that Mickey understood the meaning of such words as "potty," "pants," "wet," "dry," "pee-pee," and "poo-poo." She had brought Renée's old potty chair up from the basement and left it in the bathroom so that it could be pointed out to Mickey during the trips. He was never told, however, that he had to sit on the potty chair.

Now that Mickey had passed all of the readiness tests, Mrs. James began to prepare in earnest for the training. She began by gathering together the necessary training supplies. She had made a list of the supplies she would need, so that nothing would be forgotten.

She went to a local department store and purchased a potty chair with a plastic pot that could be easily removed by lifting it out of the chair. Although she already had the potty chair that Ronnie and Renée had used, she decided not to use it for Mickey since the pot was difficult to remove: it had to be pulled out from underneath the back of the chair. The difficulty of removing the pot would mean that Mickey wouldn't be able to empty it by himself. Finding a doll that wet was no problem; Renée had received one the previous Christmas.

At the grocery store, Mrs. James purchased Mickey's favorite snacks and drinks, especially orange soda and potato chips. He never seemed to stop asking for them. Still, she bought a wide selection, so that he would not tire of any one type. She also purchased a box of facial tissue to be kept beside the potty chair in the event that Mickey had a B.M. She would dress Mickey in Ronnie's old training pants, since they were big and baggy and would be easy for him to raise and lower. She checked off cleaning cloths and an apron with pockets from her reminder list, since she already had these items at home. Finally, she took a note pad and made up the Friends-Who-Care list. She listed the immediate family members, both sets of grandparents, a neighbor who sometimes baby-sat with Mickey, his regular baby-sitter, and Ernie and Burt from the *Sesame Street* television program.

The Training Day

That morning at breakfast, Mrs. James explained her training plans to her husband, Martin. Mr. James said he remembered how difficult everyone's life had become during the training of the other two children. He also was thinking of what a nuisance he found it to take his turn changing Mickey's diapers when he returned home all tired out from work. So he was sincere when he said, "Good luck" to his wife as he went off to work a little later that morning.

After Martin had left for work and Ronnie for school, Mrs. James took Renée over to a neighbor's house to spend the day. Now that everyone else was out of the house, she and Mickey would not be interrupted during the training period.

Mrs. James decided to conduct the training in her kitchen. The kitchen was large enough so that neither she nor Mickey would feel confined. The drinks could be kept cold in the refrigerator, and the floor was linoleum, so that any spillings or wettings could be wiped up easily. She brought the potty chair and doll into the kitchen. She lifted the pot out of the potty chair to make sure that it could be removed easily and checked to make sure the urine-signaling device was working. Then she took a piece of paper and made a reminder sheet to use during the training. On this reminder sheet she would record the time of each dry-pants inspection, prompted toileting, and accident, as a reminder to herself to conduct these various procedures. When she had finished making up the Training Reminder sheet, she went over a reminder list of questions, checking to make sure she could answer each question satisfactorily. When she encountered a question she felt unsure of, she reread the section of the procedure that answered the question. Now that she had "passed" the reminder test, she felt ready to begin Mickey's training.

Mickey was still wearing the diaper that she had put on him before breakfast. She rolled up Mickey's undershirt and pinned it so that it was about two inches above his training pants, where it would not hinder his attempts to lower or raise his pants. Mrs. James removed the diaper, told Mickey to sit on the floor, and guided his feet through the legs of a pair of old training pants. When Mickey's feet were through the pants legs, she told him to stand up. When he was standing, she told him, "Mickey, pull up your pants," guided him to bend forward slightly, and then guided his hands to the waistband of the pants. She guided his hands in grasping the waistband and then guided them in raising the pants. As he began pulling up the pants, she reduced the guidance by lifting her hands off his hands. She kept her hands close by, however, almost touching, so that she could resume the guidance should he stop. She praised him each time he attempted to raise the pants himself: "That's good, Mickey: you're pulling up your pants, like a big boy." She gave him a big hug and kiss when he had pulled the pants all the way up.

She had found it difficult to refrain from pulling up his pants for him. Although she knew that he had to learn to dress himself in order to potty independently, her natural inclination had been to do it for him, just as she had always done for Ronnie and Renée. After all, it was always faster to dress your child than to stop and wait for him to painstakingly dress himself. Fortunately, the new potty-training procedure had given her some tips on how to accomplish dressing training rapidly. And since her objective was to teach Mickey to potty by himself, she was willing to be patient and teach him to dress.

Mrs. James offered Mickey a glass of orange soda. She wanted him to drink as much as possible so that he would have the urge to urinate shortly. She had begun giving him a lot to drink at breakfast. Mickey took a sip and handed the glass back to her. She said, "Mickey, that's a good drink, isn't it? Would you like some more?" and handed the glass back to him. This time he took two sips before handing the glass back to her. She continued to praise him for drinking and continued to hand him the glass until he had drunk almost the entire glassful. She set the glass aside and said, "Mickey, let's give the doll a drink. Do you want to help the doll drink?" Mickey said yes, that he would.

Mrs. James handed him the doll and a plastic baby bottle filled with water. "Mickey, give the baby a drink. That's right. Lay her down so she can drink." When she saw that the bottle was empty, Mrs. James said, "Mickey, the dolly has to pee-pee. Let's help her sit on the potty." She picked up the doll by one of its arms and offered the doll's other arm to Mickey. After she and Mickey carried the doll to the potty, she said, "Mickey, let's help her pull down her pants." She guided him in pulling the doll's pants down. She was careful to keep the doll in a partly prone position, since the water came out when the doll was in a upright position. "Mickey, set the doll on the potty. That's right. You're a big helper."

When Mickey had placed the doll on the chair, Mrs. James told him to "Watch the dolly. The dolly is about to pee-pee." She knew the doll would begin to leak water now that it was set up straight. As the water dripped from between the doll's legs, she pointed to it and said, "Mickey, see Dolly pee-peeing in the potty." She paused a moment to make sure that Mickey was looking at the droplets of water. Then she clapped her hands and said, "Mickey, Dolly's a big girl. She's pee-peeing in the potty. Is Dolly a big girl?" Mickey nodded his head up and down and said, "Yes." Mrs. James handed Mickey a piece of candy from her apron and said, "Mickey, give the dolly a piece of candy for being such a big girl."

As Mickey held the candy to the doll's mouth, Mrs. James told him that he could eat it if he would be a big boy and go pee-pee in the potty as the dolly had. Mickey nodded his head affirmatively and ate the candy. She then said, "Mickey, Dolly is finished pee-peeing; help lift her off the potty." When they had lifted the doll from the chair, she said, "Mickey, help the dolly pull up her pants." She waited a moment before guiding his hands, to see if he would begin pulling up the doll's pants himself. He began immediately, but was having trouble pulling the pants over the doll's bottom. Mrs. James placed her hands on Mickey's to help guide him in pulling up the pants. When the pants were pulled up, Mrs. James praised him, just as she had throughout his attempts to raise the doll's pants, and then set the doll aside on the nearby kitchen table.

Then she told him, "Mickey, help the dolly by carrying her pot to the big toilet." She guided him in lifting the plastic pot from the chair. "Hold on to it tight so it won't spill." When she was sure that he had a good grip on the pot, she said, "Carry it to the big toilet in the bathroom." He started for the bathroom.

On the way to the toilet, she walked beside Mickey, always staying within arm's reach so that she could steady the pot should he start to drop it or spill its contents. When they reached the toilet, she told him, "Mickey, dump the pee-pee into the toilet." Then she guided him in turning the potty sideways so that its contents emptied into the toilet. "That's right—make sure the pee-pee is all out." She lifted her hands from his when she saw that he was following her instructions. "Now, flush the toilet." He tried to set the pot down before flushing the toilet, but she told him to hold it with his left hand and use his right hand to flush, since he was right-handed. "That's right. Put your hand on the handle. Just like Mommy does when she is finished pee-peeing."

Mickey had reached for the handle automatically. He had seen all of the family flush the toilet many times before. He had no trouble pushing the handle downward. She noticed that he seemed to enjoy flushing the toilet, probably because of the flushing noise. "Now, take the pot back to the potty." Again she remained close to him on the return trip, so as to be ready to intervene should he wish to set the pot down. When he reached the potty chair, she said, "Mickey, put the pot in the chair." He bent down and placed the pot in the chair. "Turn it around so that it fits straight. That's right," she said, as she guided his hands ever so slightly in turning the pot to its correct position.

Now she would have him inspect the doll's pants to see if they were dry. "Mickey, does Dolly have dry pants? Let's see." She guided Mickey over to the table and told him to put his hands on the doll's pants. "Why, they're dry. The dolly has dry pants. Does she have dry pants?" "Yes," he answered. "She's a big girl. Are you proud of the dolly?" she asked. Mickey nodded yes. Mrs. James continued, "Dolly has dry pants; let's give her some candy.

She's a big girl. Big girls get candy for dry pants. Mickey, can you tell her she's a big girl?" "Big girl," he said. "Here, you give the dolly candy for having dry pants." She handed Mickey a piece of candy, which he pushed toward the doll's mouth.

Then she asked him, "Mickey, do you have dry pants?" Mickey looked down at his pants. "Feel them—see if they're dry." Mickey put his hand on his pants. "Mickey, are they dry?" Mickey said, "Yes," they were. "Mickey, you're a big boy too! What do big boys get?" she asked. "Candy!" he shouted. "That's right." Making sure that his hand was still touching his pants, she told him to eat the piece of candy he was holding in his other hand. "Mickey, you're a big boy. You have dry pants. You get candy," she said. Turning from the doll she asked, "Mickey, do you want a drink?" He said, "Yes." "You do? Are your pants dry?" He felt his pants again and said very excitedly, "Dry." She handed him a glass of orange soda while saying, "Mickey, you're a big boy. You have dry pants. Big boys can have drinks." After a few swallows, he handed the glass back to her. In the next five minutes, she had Mickey check the doll's pants and then his own pants two more times, each time giving him a snack treat and then a drink of soda.

Now Mickey would learn why he should not have accidents. While he was drinking, Mrs. James spilled water on the doll's pants. Then she directed Mickey's attention to the doll. "Mickey, let's see if the dolly has dry pants. Does the doll have dry pants?" "Yes," he said. "Mickey, feel her pants," she said, guiding his hand to the doll's wet pants. He pulled his hand back when he felt the wetness. "Wet," he said. "That's right. The doll wet her pants. She's a baby," Mrs. James said sternly. "Mickey, is the dolly a baby?" Mickey nodded affirmatively. "We love Dolly but we don't want her to wet her pants. Do we love Dolly?" Mickey said, "Yes." "Do we like her to wet her pants?" "No," he answered. She was pleased by his answers. They showed that he understood that wetting was bad but that the person who wet was still loved.

"When Dolly wets her pants, she has to practice going potty," she said. "She must learn not to pee-pee in her pants. Will you help her practice?" Mickey said that yes, he would. She told him to carry the doll to the potty rapidly, to help lower her pants rapidly, to set her on the potty for a moment, to help raise her pants, and to carry her rapidly back to where she had "had the accident." Whenever necessary, Mrs. James provided instruction and manual guidance throughout the practice trials. Mickey helped the doll practice three times. For each action Mrs. James said, "Mickey, Dolly must practice fast. Help her practice fast."

After the last practice trial, she said, "Mickey, what happens when Dolly wets her pants?" He just looked at her. "She must practice," Mrs. James said. "Practice," Mickey said, looking at the doll. "What happens if you wet your pants?" she asked. "Practice," he said. "That's right. You don't want to practice, do you?" "No," he said resolutely. "Now, feel her pants. Are they wet?" she asked. "Yes," he said. "Dolly has wet pants. Do we love Dolly?" "Yes," he said. "What don't we like?" she asked. "Wet pants," he said loudly. "That's right," she said approvingly. "Mickey, are you going to wet your pants?" "No," he said. "Are you a big boy with dry pants?" He felt his pants. "Big boy," he said loudly.

"That's right—big boys have dry pants," she said. "You can have the candy. Your pants are dry." "Dry," he said, putting the candy in his mouth.

Approximately ten minutes had elapsed since the training had begun. She began asking him a series of questions, all of which were designed to inform him of how happy all his family, friends, and heroes would be when he was a big boy who could potty by himself. She also wanted to point out to him that all of these people used the toilet by themselves and thereby kept their pants dry. She wanted him to identify with and emulate these people. She began by asking, "Mickey, does Daddy wet his pants?" She had waited until he was looking at her before she asked the question; that way she could be sure that he was listening to her. Mickey shook his head and said, "No." She repeated his answer: "No, Daddy doesn't wet his pants. Daddy is a big boy. He keeps his pants dry. He pees in the potty. Does Daddy wear diapers?" "No," Mickey said. "Are you a big boy?" "Yes," Mickey answered. "Will you keep your pants dry?" "Yes," he said. "Does Ronnie wet his pants?" "No." "Does Renée wet her pants?" "No." "Does Mommy wet her pants?" "No." "Only babies wet their pants. Are you a baby?" "No." "That's right. You don't wet your pants. You're not a baby. You're a big boy!"

She would now describe to him all of the acts necessary for him to toilet himself. She would repeat this description many times that morning as a reminder of what he would be doing. She would ask him a question after each statement to ensure that he was paying attention to what she was saying. "Mickey, when you have to pee-pee, you'll go to the potty. Right?" "Yes." "Where will you go?"

129

"Potty." "You'll pull your pants down and sit on the potty. Right?" "Yes." "Then you'll pee-pee. Is that right?" "Yes," he said. "Will you pee-pee in your pants?" "No!" "And then you'll pull your pants up. Right?" "Right," he said loudly and happily. "Then you'll pick up the pot and carry it to the toilet. Right?" "Right." "Where will you carry the pot?" He pointed toward the bathroom. "Right. And dump the pee-pee in the toilet?" "Yes." "And flush the toilet?" "Yes." "Flush it just like Daddy does?" "Yes." "And then carry the pot back to the potty?" "Yes." "Where do you carry the pot?" "Potty." He pointed to the chair. "That's right, you carry it there. And put it back in the potty?" "Yes."

Now that she had had him verbally rehearse and visualize all of the toileting acts, she would suggest that he go to the potty. He had drunk over a glass of soda, so she knew he would be ready to urinate any time now. She wanted his first urination of the day to be in the potty. That would start the day's training with a success! "Mickey, sit on the potty now." She walked with Mickey over to the potty. "Mickey, pull your pants down." He looked at her, then started to sit down. "Wait, you've forgotten something." She pointed to his pants. Mickey looked down, started to reach for his pants, then stopped. She knelt down beside him and said, "Pull your pants down." He paused as if he weren't sure what to do. "Put your hands on your pants," she said again as she grasped his hands with her thumb and forefinger and guided them to the waistband of his pants. "Now, grab your pants." She placed his hands on the waistband so that his thumbs were inside next to his skin and his fingers outside, grasping the training pants. "Pull down, down," she said as she slowly guided his hands in lowering the pants about an inch. She released his hands as he began lowering the pants himself. "That's right—down past your knees. Just like a big boy!" She continued praising until he had his pants all the way down and then kissed him.

When his pants were down a few inches below his knees, she pointed to the potty chair, and he sat down. "Mickey, try and go pee-pee in the potty. Big boys pee-pee in the potty. Does Daddy pee-pee in the potty?" "Yes," he said. "Yes, he does. Well, you be a big boy too. Tell me when you pee-pee. What will you say when you pee-pee?" she asked. "Pee-pee," he answered. "That's right. You'll say pee-pee," she said. Then she stopped talking to him, because she didn't want to distract him any further. She knew that he had to relax before he could urinate; if she talked to him, he might not relax long enough to do so. After a minute or so, he started to stand up. "Wait, not yet. Sit down on the potty until you pee-pee," she said as she placed her hand on his shoulder and gently guided him back to a seated position.

I'm certainly acting differently during this training from the way I did when I trained Ronnie and Renée, she thought. Especially when I trained Ronnie; it seemed as if I were always yelling at him. Whenever he couldn't follow my instructions, which was often, I would give him the instructions again in an angry tone of voice. When he still would not follow the instructions, I would become even angrier and often spank him. I wish I had known about this physical-guidance procedure back then. I would not have gotten angry, because I could have always made sure that he followed my instruction. Even if

Mickey becomes a little difficult later, I won't let myself become angry. Rather, I'll just guide him through the task until he begins doing it himself. I think the training and especially the guidance permits a mother to be more patient. Also, my instructions this time are simpler, which should make it easier for Mickey to understand what I want him to do.

While he sat on the potty, she looked closely between his legs into the potty. Four minutes after he had been sitting, she saw him urinate. He had done it. Immediately she clapped her hands and said, "Mickey, you're a big boy! You pee-peed in the potty! I'm so proud of you!" She waited until the urine stopped, then hugged and kissed him. "You're my big boy. You pee-peed in the potty." She reached in her apron and took out a large piece of candy and handed it to him. "Here's candy for pee-peeing in the potty. Big boys get candy." He took the candy and ate it. She waited a few moments to make sure that he had finished urinating, since she didn't want him to stand up until he had finished. "Okay. You can stand up. You are finished when you pee-pee in the potty."

Mickey stood up and turned around to lift the pot out of the chair. "Wait a minute. You've forgotten something." He turned and looked at her. "Your pants," she said, pointing toward his pants. He reached down and pulled up his pants so that they were just below his buttocks. He kept pulling at the pants, but he couldn't get them up over his bottom. She reached down and took his right hand in hers. She guided his right hand from the side of his pants to the back of his pants so that he was grasping the pants with his palm facing outward.

"Mickey, pull your pants up." With his palm facing outward, the pants were pulled out from and over his bottom easily. "That's the right way to pull up your pants. Now pick up the potty." He reached down with one hand. "Use both hands so that it won't spill." He looked up at her momentarily, then placed both hands on the pot. The pot fitted tightly, but he managed to lift it from the seat. "Mickey, take it to the toilet," she said. She walked beside him, as she had done earlier when he was emptying the potty for the doll. She remained close enough to help him steady the pot, if necessary. He walked from the kitchen through the living room to the bathroom with no trouble.

The last time they were in the bathroom, she had left the toilet lid up so that it wouldn't be in the way. She was extremely pleased when he poured the contents of the pot into the toilet without being told. "Tip it over just a little bit more. That's right. Now all the pee-pee will be in the toilet." He started to set the pot on the floor. She didn't want him to do this, because he would forget to pick it up after he had flushed the toilet. She wanted him to be ready to carry the pot back to the potty chair. "Hold the potty in one hand. That's right. Now flush the toilet with your other hand. Good. That's a big boy."

As she had noticed earlier, Mickey seemed to enjoy flushing the toilet, for he smiled when he heard the flushing sound, and he had begun flushing almost before she told him to do so. He carried the pot back to the kitchen without any trouble and smiling broadly. When he reached the potty chair, he set the pot in the chair, but in a crooked position, so that it did not fit into the chair correctly. He had started to rise up and move away when Mrs. James told him, "Mickey, fix the pot so that it is straight." She bent over him and, taking his hands in hers, guided him in turning the pot around. She stopped guiding his hands as soon as he began turning the pot in the correct direction.

Once the pot was in place, she said, "Mickey, are your pants dry?" He reached down and felt the crotch of his pants with his right hand. "Dry," he said. "That's good. Your pants are dry. You're a big boy, just like Ronnie. Big boys can have a treat." She took one each of several different candies and chips from her apron and offered him his choice. "Which would you like?" He picked a corn chip. I'm glad he likes salted treats, she thought: they'll make him thirsty and he'll want more to drink. When he had eaten the corn chip, she asked him if his pants were dry and then offered him a drink. Again, as she had done with the food, she offered him his choice of milk, orange soda, cola, and fruit punch. He chose the orange soda. He took a few sips and then handed the glass back to her. After a brief moment, she handed the glass back to him and asked him if he wanted to drink some more, which he did. After he had drunk a few swallows, he said he didn't want any more. She wanted him to drink as much as possible, so she lifted the glass to her lips and said, "May I have some of your soda?" He said, "Yes." After she had pretended to drink, she handed him the glass. Much to her delight, he drank seven or eight more swallows. She recorded the time of the dry-pants inspection on her Training Reminder List so that she would be reminded in five minutes to make another inspection. She had been recording the time of each dry-pants inspection since the beginning of the training.

Since Mickey had just urinated, he wouldn't be ready to urinate again for at least fifteen minutes. In the interim before she sent him to the potty again, Mrs. James used several procedures. She used the "Friends-Who-Care" procedure to let him know how much everyone wanted to see him potty by himself. She pointed out to Mickey that all of those people toileted themselves. She wanted his identification with friends and relatives and heroes to motivate him to toilet himself. At other times, she described to him all of the various toileting acts, asking him if he would and could do them. She also continued to have him check his pants every five minutes or so and rewarded him if they were dry, with praise and a snack. Every few minutes, she offered him a choice of drinks. Each time the drinks were offered, she also checked his pants.

Almost a half-hour had passed since she had begun the training. She would now have Mickey train the doll again before sending him to the potty. That way, she might not have to use very much instruction to get him to go to the potty. After this time, the doll would be used only once more. That would be fifteen minutes later. Mrs. James felt that after Mickey had trained the doll three times, he would have a good grasp of why and how he should be toileting himself. Thus, once Mickey was sufficiently familiar with the overall training objective, she would discard the doll. After Mickey had helped the doll toilet herself, emptied her pot, given her a dry-pants check, and reacted to another accident by the doll, Mrs. James set the doll aside.

She would now send Mickey to the potty. She

would send him using some sort of general suggestion that he go rather than the direct instruction she had used the last time. If he urinated, she would reward him. If not, she would leave him on the potty for only five minutes. For each toileting act, she would use less physical guidance and direct instruction than she had the last time. Thus, Mickey would be performing each of these acts more independently each time.

She gave him the general suggestion: "Mickey, remember, big boys pee-pee in the potty. Where do big boys pee-pee?" "Potty." "You should go to the potty when you have to pee-pee." He did not move. "Is the dolly a big girl when she pee-pees in the potty?" "Yes," he said. "That's right. Can you pee-pee in the potty?" "Yes," he said, and he started pulling his pants down. He lowered them just to below his crotch and began to sit down. "Mickey, wait, pull them down a little farther." He looked at her, then down at his pants. He grasped the pants and attempted to push them down still farther. "That's right," she said. "You're pulling your pants down."

He was having difficulty, however. The pants had bunched up when he had first lowered them, making it difficult for him to lower them farther. She placed her hands on his hands, which were still grasping the waistband. She gently guided his hands in pulling the pants out from his thighs and then sliding them down. They were lowered easily to a point just above his knees. Next time he would know how to do it without her help. "That's right. You're a big boy. Big boys can pull their pants down." She had helped him lower his pants because she knew that if they were not lowered to his knees, they might bunch up when he sat down and he thus might accidentally wet them while sitting on the potty. With his pants down, he sat down by himself without being told. She was delighted; he had walked to the potty, pulled his pants down, and sat down, all without being told directly. While he sat there, she recorded the time of this prompted toileting on her Training Reminder List and then went to the refrigerator for fresh ice for his glass.

The only thing she had said to him after he sat down was that he should try and go pee-pee. Other than that, she said nothing since she didn't want to distract him. She knew that he had to relax in order to urinate; if she talked to him, he would be too interested in what she was saying to relax. She appreciated this brief respite, since it gave her time to review what had occurred so far. She spread his knees slightly apart so she could look into the pot.

Shortly after Mickey had sat down, she saw him urinate. As before, she praised, hugged, and gave him a snack. He had finished urinating, but was making no attempt to stand up. "Mickey, if you are finished pee-peeing, you can stand up," she said. He still didn't move, so she reached down and touched him lightly on the shoulder. He stood up and immediately bent over and raised his pants. Mrs. James could hardly believe her eyes. She was ecstatic. He had raised his pants without being told, and he had raised them perfectly, with no trouble and little effort. She hugged him and told him what a big boy he was. She had waited to praise him until he had finished pulling up his pants, since he was raising the pants without any help.

He turned and looked at the potty chair, then bent down and began to lift the pot from the chair. Again, he was beginning one of the toileting acts without being told. He was having a little trouble placing his fingers under the rim of the pot. She bent down and, taking his right hand, guided his fingers under one edge of the pot. With an edge to grip, he lifted the pot easily and carried it to the toilet, emptied it, flushed the toilet, brought it back to the potty chair, and reinserted it. He had needed assistance when reinserting the pot only in turning it around so that it fitted in the chair correctly. Mrs. James's heart was pounding; he had done so much by himself. He had learned the entire sequence for emptying the pot. It could be only a matter of time now before he pottied himself. Now she would have to remember to praise him only at the completion of the pottying sequence, since she did not want to distract him while he was doing so well.

During the next fifteen minutes she gave him three pants checks—one every five minutes—and continued to talk to him about the benefits of toileting himself and how happy everyone would be with his newfound skill. He had begun to drink less, so she began offering the drinks more often and varying the types of drinks. He had gone to the potty again when she had asked him to show her his potty. He had walked over to it and touched it and then begun lowering his pants. He had lowered his pants by himself and had sat down on the potty chair. We're getting close, she thought; now he can raise and lower his pants by himself. He also knows how to empty the pot by himself. He urinated within a minute after sitting down. Mrs. James was extremely pleased that he had urinated so soon after sitting down. This meant that he had learned what he was to do in the potty. Now all he had to do was go to the potty without her telling him to and he would be trained.

One hour had passed since she had begun the training. Mickey had finished working with the doll. Three times with the doll seemed just about right; during this last session with the doll he had seemed to be losing interest in training it. After he had trained the doll, she asked him where he went potty. The question produced an immediate response: he walked over to the potty. Although he lowered his pants and sat down willingly, he did not urinate. She let him sit there for five minutes and then motioned to him to stand up. Her reasoning was that if he had not urinated within five minutes, he probably was not going to urinate for a while. There were two possibilities as to why he had not urinated at this time: he had developed bladder control and was merely waiting to urinate later, or he had not been drinking as much liquid as he had earlier and did not have the urge to urinate. She made a mental note to begin using salted peanuts and corn chips at the dry-pants checks as a means of increasing his desire to drink.

Within every fifteen-minute period, she had continued to talk about the advantages of self-toileting, how Mickey would be like all his favorite people when he pottied himself, and how happy all these people would be when he was a big boy. She continued to describe all the things he would be doing when he pottied himself: lowering and raising his own pants, urinating in the potty, removing and emptying the pot, and replacing it in the chair. She also asked him two other questions: "Where is your potty?" which required him to walk over and touch it or just to point at the potty, and 2) "Where do you go when you have to pee-pee?," to which he replied, "Potty."

Another fifteen minutes had elapsed. It had been thirty minutes since Mickey had urinated. She wanted him to go to the potty in the next minute or so. She would do so by giving him a dry-pants check, which she hoped would serve as a general suggestion to go potty himself. She was about to give him the dry-pants check when he began pacing and grabbing his crotch. "Do you have to pee-pee?" she asked. "No," he said. "Are you sure?" "Yes," he said, turning away so that his back was to her. She suspected that he was about to wet his pants.

She was walking toward him when she noticed urine running down his leg. "No, Mickey" she said loudly. "Don't wet your pants." She grasped his shoulders and turned him around so that he was facing her. Looking directly at him, she said, "Mickey, you should not wet your pants. Big boys don't wet their pants. I love you, but I don't like wet pants." There was no trace of anger in her voice. She did not want him to think that she was terribly upset with him as a person, but rather that she was disappointed that he had wet his pants.

She saw that his pants were soaked and that he had made a small puddle on the floor. "You'll have to clean it up," she said in an even tone, pointing to the puddle. She gently guided him over to the kitchen table, where she had placed some old rags for him to use in cleaning up any accidents. "Mickey, pick up the rag." He made no attempt to grasp the rag, so she rapidly guided his hand in picking up the rag. "Carry the rag to the puddle," she said, as she began rapidly guiding him to the puddle. As he began walking briskly, she eliminated the guidance, but re-

mained within reach so that she could reapply the
guidance if necessary. At the puddle, she guided
him to a kneeling position so that he could wipe it
up more easily. "Mickey, wipe up the puddle." She
guided his hand in a wiping motion, and as he began
wiping, she lifted her hands from his. When he had
finished wiping, she told him to carry the rag to a
plastic bucket that was located beside the kitchen
table. He walked over to the bucket without any
guidance. When he was standing beside the bucket,
she told him to drop the rag in the bucket, which
he did. "Mickey, you wet your pants. You must
practice going to the potty fast," she said, guiding
him back to the spot where he had wet his pants.
She put the flat of her hand against his back when
guiding him to walk. She wanted him to walk
briskly during his required practice.

When they reached the location of his accident,
she oriented him so that he was facing the potty
chair. "Mickey, practice walking to the potty. Practice fast." He looked up at her and his face con-
torted as if he were going to cry. "You shouldn't
cry," she said. "You remember when you had Dolly
practice after she wet her pants?" "Yes," he said.
"Well, you must practice when you wet your pants.
Just the way you had Dolly practice when she wet
her pants. You must practice so you will learn not to
wet your pants. I want you to pee-pee in the potty
and have dry pants because I love you. The practice
shows you where you should pee-pee."

Her explanation seemed to make sense to him,
for he said, "Okay," and his face relaxed. "Mickey,
practice walking to the potty," she said. She hesitated
just a moment to see if he was going to move. He
did not, so she guided him rapidly to the potty chair.

"Practice pulling your pants down. Practice fast." He began lowering his pants, but not as rapidly as she wanted him to, so she began guiding him rapidly. Since he was still not moving as rapidly as she wished, she had to give him almost total guidance, whenever he began lowering the pants himself. With her guiding him, his pants were lowered quickly.

"Mickey, practice sitting on the potty," she said. "Practice sitting fast." He made no effort to sit, so she guided him in sitting down on the potty chair. His bottom had barely touched the seat when she said, "Practice standing up. Practice fast" and gently but rapidly guided him back to a standing position. "Practice pulling up your pants. Practice fast." He began raising his pants but was dawdling along, so she began to guide his hands rapidly. He seemed to dislike the guidance, for he began to raise the pants rapidly himself—at which point she ceased guiding him, but kept her hands close by in case he should stop. When the pants were raised, she guided him rapidly to a corner of the kitchen opposite the potty chair.

When they reached the corner, she said, "Mickey, practice walking to the potty. Practice walking fast." She repeated the same sequence: Mickey was required to walk rapidly to the potty, pull his pants down rapidly, sit just a brief moment on the potty, raise his pants rapidly, and then walk rapidly to another room in the house, where the practice would begin again. She had Mickey practice going to the potty a total of ten times—each time from a different room or a different location in a room in the house.

The marvel of this required practice, she thought,

is that I'm teaching Mickey what he should have done instead of wetting his pants, and he's learning to find the potty from any location in the house. Learning to walk to the potty from anywhere in the house will be of value to him once he is trained. Mickey had needed some manual guidance throughout the first couple of practice trials, but had carried out all the instructions very rapidly thereafter without any guidance.

Wiping up the puddle and the ten practice trials had taken about ten minutes. Now Mrs. James would give Mickey ten dry pants checks while he was still in his wet pants and then have him change into dry pants so that she could begin the training again. As soon as the tenth practice trial ended, she said, "Mickey, are your pants dry?" He looked at her and shook his head up and down indicating that yes, they were. "No, your pants are wet," she said softly but firmly, taking his hand and placing it on the crotch of his pants. Using the Friends-Who-Care list, she began telling Mickey that each person on the list did not like wet pants, but did like dry pants. "Mickey, Daddy doesn't like wet pants. Are your pants wet? Feel your pants," she said, gently guiding his hand to the wet spot on the pants. "Daddy likes dry pants, not wet pants." Then she began the second dry-pants check. "Mickey, Mommy doesn't like wet pants. Are your pants wet? Feel your pants," she said, guiding his hand to his pants. "Mickey, Mommy likes dry pants, not wet pants. Mickey, Ronnie doesn't like wet pants," etc. She used a different person from the list for each check until ten checks had been made. She finished the tenth check by saying, "Big boys don't wet their pants. Big boys have dry pants."

Fifteen minutes had elapsed since his accident. During that time, she had required Mickey to clean up his puddle and to practice going to the potty ten times, and had pointed out to him that each of his loved ones did not like wet pants. Mrs. James now began the last phase of the accident procedure. She said, "Mickey, take off your wet pants." He pulled his pants down to his knees by himself. He had some difficulty lowering the pants—since they were wet, they stuck to his skin—but he got them down. "Now sit on the floor and pull your .pants off," she said firmly. He sat down, raised his knees toward his chest, and began pulling off the pants. He got the pants off and started to hand them to her. "Mickey," she said, "put the pants down." He set the pants on the floor. "Mickey, go to the table and get some dry pants." She walked beside him to the table. He picked up the dry pants and turned toward her as if he were asking her to put them on for him. "Mickey, sit down," she said, motioning toward the floor. After he sat down, she guided his feet through the pant legs. "Mickey, pull your pants up." He pulled them up to his knees. "Now stand up. Pull your pants up all the way," she said. She was pleased that he pulled them up without assistance. "Mickey, pick up your wet pants. Carry the wet pants to the bathroom," she told him. He carried them to the bathroom as she walked behind him. When he reached the bathroom, she told him to lay the pants on the side of the bathtub, where they could dry. Then they walked back to the kitchen together.

Mrs. James was not dismayed that he had had an accident. She realized that he had to learn not to have accidents and that the only way he could learn this was to find out what would happen when he did have an accident. He might have had the accident in order to find out how she would react to him. Or, he might have been curious to see if he would receive the same treatment that he had given the doll when she had wet. That was what she liked so much about the doll: Mickey could not be surprised by what happened to him following his accident because he had already seen what happened to the doll when she had an accident. Also, she knew that the purpose of the training was to teach Mickey how to potty by himself, as well as to motivate him to continue to use the potty in order to avoid wetting his pants. The training procedures were teaching Mickey to be responsible for his own toileting. Part of this newly acquired responsibility was learning that he had become responsible for his accidents.

When they reached the kitchen, Mrs. James immediately gave Mickey a dry-pants check. "Mickey, do you have dry pants?" He reached down and felt his pants. "Dry," he exclaimed proudly. "Big boys have dry pants," she said. "You can have a drink. Do you want some orange soda?" "Yes," he said, smiling from ear to ear. He took the glass and drank several ounces. After the dry pants inspection, she began asking him a series of questions. "Mickey, are you going to wet your pants again?" "No," he said resolutely, shaking his head from side to side. "Where will you go pee-pee?" "Potty," he answered. "That's right: big boys pee-pee in the potty. Where do big boys pee-pee?" "Potty," he said. "Don't wet your pants. If you wet your pants, you'll have to practice going to the potty. What happens if you wet your pants?" "Practice," he said, pursing his lips together. "That's right: you have to practice when you wet your pants."

In the next ten minutes she gave him two more pants checks while also offering him as much to drink as he wanted. After the last drink she said, "Remember, if you want to keep your pants dry, you must pee-pee in the potty." She had barely spoken the words when he walked over to the potty, lowered his pants, and sat down. Within a few moments he said, "Pee-pee," while pointing toward the pot.

"Did you pee-pee?" she asked. "Yes," he said with a smile. Sure enough, the pot was filled with urine. She applauded, hugged and praised him, and gave him a big piece of apple, his favorite fruit. She also offered him a glass of punch, which he drank eagerly. He handed the glass back to her, then stood up and raised his pants. He turned around, lifted the pot from the chair, and carried it to the toilet.

In the bathroom, Mickey emptied the contents of the pot into the toilet and flushed it; then he carried the pot back to the chair, where he reinserted it. He has just about got it, she thought happily.

Two hours had now passed since she had begun the training. Mickey had urinated two more times, following a general suggestion that he keep his pants dry. He could perform everything for himself: lowering and raising his pants; walking to, and sitting on, the potty chair; removing the pot; emptying the pot into the toilet; flushing the toilet; and replacing the pot. All that was left was for him to go to the potty without any suggestion of any sort that he do so. She had ceased giving him instructions to go to the potty over an hour ago. Now he was going to the potty whenever a general comment about toileting coincided with his urge to urinate. As a result, he was going to the potty about every twenty minutes. Her general comments included describing the advantages of staying dry, asking him where he would pee-pee should he need to urinate, and continuing to mention all his favorite people who used the toilet by themselves. Because of his responsiveness to these general suggestions, she knew that he would go to the potty by himself very soon.

Her hopes were soon realized. She had just given Mickey a drink at one of the dry-pants checks and was setting the glass on the table when she saw him walking over to the potty chair. He pulled down his pants and sat on the potty. This is it, she thought, he has gone to the potty by himself. She walked over to him, knelt down, and watched closely between his legs to see whether or not he would urinate. Then began the sweetest sound she had ever heard. "Pee-pee, potty!" he said. He had urinated in the potty. "You're my big boy!" she said joyfully. "You went potty all by yourself!" Mickey was smiling from ear to ear and saying, "Potty!" She clapped her hands, then hugged and kissed him. She gave him several pieces of candy and a slice of apple, which he ate slowly but with obvious enjoyment. She didn't want to instruct him to stand when he had finished, preferring, instead, that he stand up by himself. "When you are through pee-peeing, you can get up."

Mickey remained on the potty a few moments, then stood up and raised his pants. He started to walk toward her. "Mickey, what have you forgotten?" she asked. He turned, looked at the potty chair, and went over and removed the pot. She remained in the kitchen while he carried the pot to the bathroom. She wanted to see if he could carry out the emptying and flushing without her being present, since the time was rapidly approaching when he would be expected to carry out all these tasks in her absence; remaining in the kitchen was her way of starting him on the road to independence. The sound of the flushing toilet and his arrival back in the kitchen holding the empty pot signified that he had emptied the pot successfully. He walked over to the potty chair and reinserted the pot without difficulty. She praised him: "Mickey, you're a big boy. You dumped the pot by yourself."

The turning point in training had been reached: Mickey had gone to the potty all by himself. She was not yet ready to terminate the training, however, since she wanted to be sure that his newly demonstrated skills would be maintained. Accordingly, she would now make a few changes in the procedure to ensure that Mickey would continue to toilet himself after the training ended. On his next few toiletings she would not give him candy following a urination, so that he would no longer expect to be rewarded for the act of urination. However, she would continue to praise him after he had reinserted the pot—which, of course, was the last step in the toileting sequence. She did not want him to become dependent upon snacks; otherwise, he would expect someone to give him a snack each time he urinated. Rather, she wanted him to expect to be praised for keeping his pants dry. She knew that if he kept his pants dry, then he must be going to the potty when he needed to urinate.

Prior to Mickey's first self-initiation, Mrs. James had been checking his pants every five minutes. But here again something must be done so that he did not come to expect someone to check his pants every five minutes. So now she would begin lengthening the period between dry-pants checks to a point that seemed compatible with her and the family's daily routine. She would begin by giving a pants check every fifteen minutes, then every thirty minutes, every hour, and finally every two hours.

She now brought in several of his toys for him to play with. Since he had gone to the potty by himself, she wanted to introduce objects with which he could become preoccupied. Now he would have to leave the toys in order to urinate. It was a stern test, but a necessary one, since many occasions would arise after training in which he would have to decide for himself to leave an entertaining activity and go to the potty.

The focus of her dialogue now changed somewhat. The emphasis became, in effect, that Mickey now had proved that he was a big boy by pottying himself and that he should continue to do so. She began comparing him to all of his favorite people. "Mickey, you're a big boy just like Daddy and Ronnie. You don't need diapers anymore. Only babies wear diapers. You're not a baby. Mommy is so proud of you. You potty all by yourself." Lastly, she wanted to be able to watch him go to the toilet by himself a few more times, so that she was sure that he could and would continue to perform all the various toileting acts by himself.

The one part of the procedure that would not be altered was the frequent offering of drinks. Mickey had to continue to drink in order to keep his urge to urinate at a high level. Thus, following his first independent toileting she continued to offer him a wide and frequent choice of drinks.

Mrs. James called her husband at work a few minutes after Mickey's first independent toileting. She told her husband the good news and had him talk to Mickey. Mickey became very much excited during the conversation, telling his daddy, "I potty, myself. Big boy. Dry pants."

About twenty minutes after his first independent toileting, Mickey went to the potty again by himself. Mrs. James was amused when she saw him begin lowering his pants even though he was still a few feet from the potty chair. She remembered that Ronnie and Renée had done the same thing. When he urinated a few minutes later, she said, "That's good," and clapped her hands. She did not give him any candy, however. Much to her delight, he did not ask for any candy, but rather went about his business: raising his pants, lifting the pot from the chair, emptying the urine into the toilet, and then reinserting the pot in the chair.

After he had reinserted the pot, he came over to her with his arms outstretched. He always did this when he wanted her to hold him. "You want me to hold you? Are your pants dry?" He felt his pants and said loudly, "Dry." "Your pants are dry," she said, feeling them. "Come sit on my lap. You have dry pants. My dress won't get wet." While she held him on her lap, she continued to discuss his new toileting skills. Every few minutes she would pick up a glass from the table and offer him a drink.

After about ten minutes, he climbed down from her lap and went over to the potty chair and urinated. He also had a B.M. She had placed facial tissue beside the potty chair in anticipation of just such an event. She knew that he had had a B.M. when he turned around before raising his pants, pointed at the pot, and said, "Poo-poo, poo-poo." She walked over, saw that he had had a B.M., and said, "You're a big boy. Big boys poo-poo in the potty. You're just like Daddy and Ronnie. You make

Mommy very happy." Then she said, "Mickey, wipe yourself." He took a piece of tissue and wiped himself. He knew what to do; she had shown him before how to wipe when he had dirtied his diapers. He probably hasn't done a very thorough wiping job, she thought, but all I care about right now is that he learn to wipe himself after a B.M. I won't always be around to help him wipe, since he is now pottying himself. Besides, I can check his bottom every day at bathtime, in case he hasn't done a complete job. Mickey placed the soiled tissue in the pot, then pulled up his pants. That little character, she thought: he knows just what to do. She followed him to the toilet this time to make sure that he emptied everything into the toilet. He did, so she didn't interfere. When he had replaced the pot, she praised him for being a big boy.

During the next thirty minutes, Mickey went to the potty and urinated twice. He had now gone to the potty by himself a total of five times. Mrs. James decided that Mickey had successfully completed his toilet training. It had taken her a little more than three hours to teach Mickey to toilet himself. It was lunchtime, but she decided first to call her monther and give her the good news. Turning to Mickey, she said, "Mickey, let's call Grandma and tell her that you can potty by yourself." Mickey said, "Yes" and clapped his hands.

On the phone, Mickey's grandmother said she was absolutely stunned by the speed with which Mickey had been trained. Mrs. James reflected the same sentiment: "Yes, I was surprised that the training worked at all with Mickey. I had figured that he wouldn't like it or that I would probably do something wrong. I still can't quite believe that it went so well. . . . Yes, he's completely trained—he goes all by himself. . . . The potty chair? The nicest thing about the potty chair was that he could remove the pot by himself and dump his pee-pee in the toilet.

"The doll? Yes, I think it helped him to learn by first training the doll. Actually, you need all the various procedures to make it work. . . . No, he didn't tantrum very much except for a little bit after he had an accident, when I had him clean up his accident and practice going to the potty. . . . Yes, he really enjoyed the training. I thought he might get tired, but it was really a pleasant experience for both of us. I don't remember when he and I have spent so much concentrated time together.

"Oh, I'm sure the training effects will last. You see, I'll be checking his pants several times each day for the first couple of days. . . . When? Well, before he eats, goes to bed, when Ronnie comes home from school, and when Martin gets home from work. . . . Yes, I'm going to get the whole family involved. Everyone will be checking Mickey's pants and praising him if they're dry. I've made myself a reminder list to use during the next week. . . . Well, I've listed on it all the times each day that I just told you about. You know—meals, bedtime. I'll check the times off after I check Mickey's pants. That way I won't forget to make the checks.

"An accident? Well, if he has an accident, he'll have to change his own pants, clean up any wet spots on the floor, and practice going to the potty ten times from different rooms in the house. Right. He doesn't like the practice or the cleaning up. I guess the thought of having to do it keeps him from wetting his pants. Come to think of it, I guess the idea of having to clean your clothes is part of what makes adults toilet correctly. Well, I've got to go now. It's time to fix lunch. 'Bye."

Mrs. James returned the doll to Renée's room and the extra training pants to Mickey's room and put the drinks and snacks away. She wiped off the table and then began making lunch. Mickey was in his room playing with his toys. She carried the potty into his room so that it would be available if he should need it.

When lunch was prepared, she told Mickey to come and eat. She picked him up and set him in his high chair. She brought lunch over to him and said, "Mickey, are your pants dry?" He reached down, touched his pants, and said, "Dry." "You're a big boy. You have dry pants. You can eat your lunch. Now all the family has dry pants when they eat," she said, setting down his plate. While Mickey ate, she called her neighbor and asked her to bring Renée home.

When the neighbor arrived with Renée, Mrs. James said, "Mickey is a big boy. He can go to the potty by himself. Renée, can you tell Mickey that he is a big boy?" Renée said, "Mickey is a big boy." "That's right," stressed Mrs. James: "he can potty by himself." The neighbor walked over, bent down and put her arm around Mickey's shoulder, and said, "You're such a big boy. I can hardly believe that you use the potty all by yourself."

At these words, Mrs. James smiled to herself. Her neighbor had always claimed that potty training was not a problem. She had always been somewhat critical of the potty-training methods Mrs. James had used with Ronnie and Renée. She had claimed to have trained her own children by the age of 16 months. What she had meant, of course, was that they would urinate in the potty if she placed them there every hour. Actually, the neighbor's children had not gone to the potty by themselves until they were almost three years old. Yet this woman had always criticized Mrs. James for her inability to train Ronnie and Renée at an early age. Well, I guess I've gotten the last laugh, Mrs. James thought, to her immense pleasure.

After lunch, Mrs. James worked around the house while Renée and Mickey played in the backyard. Mrs. James had set the potty chair in the backyard in case Mickey needed to use it. Every hour or so she would walk up to Mickey and ask him if his pants were dry. He would look down at his pants, touch them, and say very proudly, "Dry." She praised him: "Mickey, you have dry pants. That's good," and then went back into the house. At 3 P.M. she took a snack out to Renée and Mickey. She showed Mickey the snack, then asked if his pants were dry. Since they were, she gave him the snack without delay and praised and hugged him.

When Ronnie came home from school, she told him the good news. Ronnie loved his little brother very much and became quite elated. She told Ronnie to ask Mickey if his pants were dry. Ronnie asked Mickey, who excitedly answered, "Dry." Ronnie, with his mother's prompting, then told Mickey, "You're a big boy like me." Mickey said, "Like Ronnie." "Yes," Ronnie answered, "just like me." The scene was repeated when Mr. James arrived home from work. Mickey ran up to him at the doorway and shouted excitedly, "Daddy, me dry, me dry." Mr. James picked him up, felt his pants, and said, "Now I have two big boys with dry pants, Ronnie and Mickey."

154

Mickey going to the potty all by himself.

That night, just before supper, Mr. James asked Mickey if his pants were dry. Since they were, she said, "Mickey, you have dry pants. Daddy and I and Renée and Ronnie have dry pants. Let's all sit down and have supper." Several times that evening, different family members asked Mickey if he had dry pants. He had gone to the potty several times since the training had ended. Mrs. James had instructed the family not to praise him excessively for going to the potty, but rather to say, "That's nice— you're keeping your pants dry." She wanted him to receive approval and attention for having dry pants, not for toileting himself.

She checked his pants once more just before he went to bed. She decided not to put him in diapers that night; instead, she placed a rubberized sheet under his top sheet and dressed him in training pants. It really would have made no difference, she knew, if she had put a diaper on him that night, but she wanted to avoid ever having to dress him again in diapers. After he was in bed, she showed the family the Training Reminder List that she had used. "He was trained in less than four hours," she told them proudly. She also showed them the After-Training Reminder List that she would be using the first week after training. It would serve simply as a reminder to check Mickey's pants several times during the day. After the first week it would no longer be necessary to check his pants with any regularity, other than to comment occasionally on how nice it was that he had dry pants. Then she showed Mickey's diploma. "See this: Mickey gets a diploma for having graduated from potty training,"

By virtue of the authority vested in her

as potty trainer,

Lee James

Trainer's name

has conferred on

Mickey James

Child's name

22 months

Child's age

The degree of P.T. (Potty-Trained)

and has granted this Diploma

as evidence this _9_ day of _May_, 19 _73_

day   month   year

Thereof

Lee James   _Martin James_

Mother   Father

Mickey's diploma.

she told Ronnie and Renée. "Daddy and I are going to fill it out right now."

After Ronnie and Renée were in bed, Mrs. James discussed her post-training plans with her husband. "I've got to keep him in clothes that he can lower and raise easily," she said. "I'll use pants with elastic waistbands and avoid pants with belts, zippers, and snaps until I've taught him how to undo and redo them." "Is there anything else special that we have to do?" he asked. "Yes—we should make sure that the potty is always available to him. If I take him downtown, I'll take the pot in the car. If we go to Pat and Barbara's, we'll take the potty chair to their house. When we barbecue in the backyard and eat at the picnic table, we'll take the potty chair outside with us. To make sure that he knows where it is, we'll have him help put it there." "What if he wets his pants?" he asked. "Oh, one of us will have him clean up any wet spots he might have made. Then we'll have him practice going back and forth to the potty ten times from different spots in the house. And finally, he'll have to change himself." "Honey, you did a great job today," he said, taking her hand and patting it. "I know," she said. "I just wish I'd known about this procedure six years ago when I was trying to train Ronnie. I kept thinking all day, where was this procedure when I needed it then?"

CHAPTER 7

Reminder List

This chapter contains several types of reminders about training for you to use during training, after training, and in preparing for training. Before training, read the Reminder Questions on the next page and try to answer them, holding a piece of paper over each answer. Do not start to train if you find yourself having difficulty in answering the questions yourself. Instead, read this manual over again carefully until you are able to answer the questions correctly. These Reminder Questions and their answers also serve as a summary review of the procedure which you can glance at quickly during, as well as shortly before, training. A Reminder List of Supplies is given on page 172. This list is to be used before training to assist you in gathering all of the items you will need. A Reminder Sheet for Prompting and Inspections is printed on pages 173-74. You should use this list to remind yourself during training as to when you should prompt your child to toilet himself and when to inspect his pants. You will use the Reminder Sheet for After-Training Pants Inspections (page 175) to remind yourself after training as to when you should inspect your child's pants. For convenience, you may wish to copy the Reminder Sheets for Prompting and Inspections,

Supplies, and After-Training Pants Inspections so that you will have the lists in front of you when you need them.

QUESTIONS AND ANSWERS

Before training, read and answer the following questions. If you have difficulty in answering them, do not start to train until you have read this manual again.

1. Q. Which room of the house should I use for training?
   A. If possible, the kitchen.
2. Q. Should I have a friend or family members watch?
   A. No. Only the trainer and her assistant (if any) should be present.
3. Q. Should I create a strict and severe atmossphere?
   A. No. Be cheerful and enthusiastic.
4. Q. What supplies will I need before starting?
   A. A doll, a well-designed potty chair, training pants, drinks, snacks, Reminder Lists, and an apron with pockets.
5. Q. Should I use different types of drinks?
   A. Yes, several types.
6. Q. What are some of the types of snacks I should use?
   A. Candy, cookies, potato chips, sugared cereal, pieces of fruit.
7. Q. Should I use all of the recommended procedures, or can I omit some?
   A. Use all of them.

8. Q. How can I tell whether my child has enough bladder control to be trained?

A. He has bladder control if he urinates large amounts at one time and stays dry for hours in between.

9. Q. How can I tell if my child has enough instructional readiness for toilet training?

A. Give the test for following instructions.

10. Q. If my child is stubbon about following any instructions, what should I do?

A. Teach him to follow your instructions before you try to toilet-train him.

11. Q. Can I do anything to make my child more ready for training?

A. Yes. Let him watch you toilet, teach him to lower and raise his pants, teach necessary words, and teach him to obey.

12. Q. Should I try using the old-style method of training before trying this new method?

A. No. If the old-style method fails, the new method will take extra time.

13. Q. I've had bad luck twice in training my child. Should I try again, or should I have my husband try it?

A. It probably would be easier if your husband tries it.

14. Q. My child seems to have trouble in trying to urinate. What should I do?

A. See your doctor.

15. Q. What kind of potty chair should I use?

A. A type that has a pot that is removed from the top of chair.

16. Q. What kind of doll should I use?

A. The type that wets.

17. Q. What is the Friends-Who-Care-list?

A. A list of people and fictional characters whom your child loves and respects.

18. Q. Should I let my child watch television when he's not busy during training?
A. No.

19. Q. Suppose the phone rings. What should I do?
A. Tell the caller you will call back later or do not answer.

20. Q. What should I do about the training pants I use during training?
A. Make sure the leg and waist openings are very loose.

21. Q. How often do I make a pants inspection?
A. About every five minutes.

22. Q. How do I make sure my child understands the difference between wet and dry pants?
A. Have him touch his pants during the pants inspection and say "dry" or "wet."

23. Q. How do I make sure that my child will urinate during training if training lasts only a few hours?
A. You give him many extra drinks.

24. Q. How much do I give my child to drink?
A. Encourage him to drink *at least* one cup during each hour.

25. Q. Suppose my child won't drink much. What can I do?
A. Use imitation, tasty drinks, salty foods, and "priming."

26. Q. What should I do if my child starts talking about the weather?
A. Change the topic immediately back to toilet training.

27. Q. Should I use manual guidance?

A. Yes, whenever your child does not or cannot follow an instruction.

28. Q. Do I grasp my child firmly when I guide his hands?

A. No—grasp as gently as possible.

29. Q. Where should I be when I give my child instructions?

A. Within easy arm's reach, so that you can manually guide him without delay. Make sure that he is looking at you before giving him an instruction.

30. Q. How long do I wait after I give the instructions before I use manual guidance?

A. About two seconds.

31. Q. For which actions should I use manual guidance?

A. All actions for which you give instructions.

32. Q. Do I always stand right next to my child when I give an instruction?

A. No—only until he has followed that instruction a few times without the need for manual guidance.

33. Q. Should the doll that I use be dressed in any way?

A. Yes, in training pants.

34. Q. What should I have the doll do?

A. All of the actions needed to toileting: pants lowering, urinating, etc.

35. Q. Do I have my child watch while I guide the doll?

A. No—have your child "teach" the doll to toilet by guiding her himself.

36. Q. Do I have the doll empty the potty and flush it?

A. No—have your child do this.

37. Q. Should I allow the doll to have an accident in her pants?

A. Yes, and have your child "discover" the accident and correct the doll.

38. Q. How long should I use the doll?

A. Until your child is able to "train" her correctly.

39. Q. How often do I give my child a practice toileting trial at the start of training?

A. About every fifteen minutes at the start.

40. Q. When do I make the prompted toileting trials less frequent?

A. When he stops needing manual guidance and instructions.

A. When he has had two or three urinations in the potty, one each prompted trial?

A. About ten minutes at first.

42. Q. When should I shorten the time I require him to sit on the potty?

A. When he has had two or three urinations in the potty, one of which occurs quickly.

43. Q. If my child goes to the potty without being told to, how long should he sit there?

A. At that stage, let him decide.

44. Q. What is the first type of reminder I use to him to go to the potty?

A. A direct instruction.

45. Q. Once he walks to the potty when I give a direct instruction, what kind of reminder do I use on the next trial?

A. A general question as to whether he wants to go.

46. Q. Once he has gone to the potty when I have just asked if he wanted to, then what do I do on the next trial?

A. Just remind him about the function of the potty.

47. Q. If my child fidgets about or looks as if he needs to urinate, what do I do?

A. Give him a toileting reminder.

48. Q. What do I do when my child sits on the potty for the first time?

A. Praise and reassure him.

49. Q. What do I do if he tries to get up from the potty?

A. Use gentle manual guidance and instructions to keep him seated.

50. Q. What do I do if he is active and restless while sitting on the potty?

A. Instruct him to relax, and praise him when he is even partly relaxed.

51. Q. What do I do if my boy's urine misses the potty?

A. Next time have him lean slightly forward.

52. Q. What do I do if my child starts playing with his genitals while sitting on the pot?

A. Distract him casually with conversation or a toy.

53. Q. What are the types of approval I should give my child to motivate him?

A. 1) verbal (praise), 2) gestural (hugs, etc.), 3) Friends-Who-Care procedure, 4) snack items, and 5) extra drinks.

54. Q. Do I exhibit this approval all the time?

A. No; show the approval for specific actions.

55. Q. Do I say anything when I show approval for what he did?

A. Yes; always tell him why you are so pleased.

56. Q. In first teaching a new toileting action, when do I show approval?

A. When he first starts the action, continuing through its completion.

57. Q. Do I still show approval for an action if he required some manual guidance to do it?

A. Yes—show approval at those moments when he was trying.

58. Q. After he has done the toileting action once or twice, when do I show approval?

A. Only at the completion of the action.

59. Q. Do I continue showing approval throughout training for his toileting?

A. No; fade out the approval until finally no approval is given for toileting.

60. Q. If I give no approval for toileting, when should I give approval?

A. During the pants inspections, for having stayed dry.

61. Q. Do I use the Friends-Who-Care approval at the very start of training?

A. Yes.

62. Q. At what moments do I mention the friends listed on the Friends-Who-Care list?

A. Whenever you give approval.

63. Q. Should I mention every friend who is on the Friends-Who-Care list?

A. Yes—one or two at a given time.

64. Q. When I speak to my child to tell him what he is supposed to do, how can I make sure that he is listening to me?

A. Call him by name.

65. Q. Should I always call him by name before I start talking to him?

A. Yes.

66. Q. If he still does not seem to be paying atten-

tion to me after I have called him by name, what do I do?

A. Orient his face toward you and repeat your statement.

67. Q. How can I make sure that my child understands what I'm saying?

A. Ask him a question about what you have said.

68. Q. Should I always ask him a question right after I have told him something?

A. Yes.

69. Q. What do I do if he answers my question incorrectly and I know he was paying attention?

A. Tell him the answer; then repeat the question.

70. Q. What do I do if he does answer my question correctly?

A. Show your visible delight and approval for his understanding.

71. Q. If my child doesn't speak, how can I have him answer my questions?

A. Ask only questions that can be answered by a head shake or a head nod or by pottying.

72. Q. What is Verbal Rehearsal?

A. Telling your child how to potty, what benefits result from pottying, and what disappointments result from accidents.

73. Q. Do I start using this Verbal Rehearsal at the very start of training?

A. Yes, right after you have finished with the Doll-That-Wets procedure.

74. Q. When do I talk to my child with this Verbal Rehearsal procedure?

A. During any free time when he is not actively practicing the toileting actions.

75. Q. Do I talk to him at all about anything except pottying?

A. No.

76. Q. Suppose he starts talking about something besides pottying?

A. Immediately change the conversation to the Verbal Rehearsal of pottying.

77. Q. When his answers indicate that he does understand how he is supposed to potty and why he should potty, do I stop the Verbal Rehearsal of pottying?

A. No: be repetitious, noting all of the different advantages, situations, and people who are involved in pottying.

78. Q. Which part of the pottying actions should I emphasize in my Verbal Rehearsal?

A. The parts that he seems to have the most trouble with.

79. Q. When I give my child instructions to do something, should my statement be brief or lengthy?

A. Be brief.

80. Q. When I give him instructions, should I give the details of what I want?

A. Yes, if he has not done it before.

81. Q. When should I make my instructions to him more general and omit the details?

A. As he shows that he can follow the more detailed instructions.

82. Q. Should I use gestures whenever I tell him to do some pottying action?

A. Yes, especially if he is very young.

83. Q. Should he wear trousers or slacks during training?

A. No, just underpants.

84. Q. Should he be wearing a shirt during training? What kind?

A. No, unless you roll up and pin the bottom or unless it is very short.

85. Q. What type of underpants should he wear?

A. Pants with very loosely fitting waist and big leg openings.

86. Q. Should I teach him to pull up his pants the way a grownup does, by grasping the two sides of the pants?

A. No. Have one of his hands grasp the front, the other the back of the pants.

87. Q. What are the four steps I should take when my child wets his pants, and in what order?

A. 1) Give verbal disapproval, 2) Require practice in pottying, 3) Give the wet-pants-awareness trials, 4) Have him change his pants.

88. Q. Do I have him finish urinating in the pot when I catch him wetting his pants?

A. No.

89. Q. What type of disapproval do I show for an accident?

A. Verbal disapproval, without anger.

90. .Q. During the Positive Practice after an accident: a) how many trials should I give? b) Where should each trial start? c) What should I say? d) How fast should he go? e) Do I allow time for him to urinate? f) Suppose he does not do what I say?

A. a) Give ten trials, performed very rapidly. b) Start each trial from a distant location.

c) Tell him only that he must practice potty-ing and describe what he must do. d) He should move rapidly throughout each action. e) No. Have him seated on the potty only for an instant. f) Manually guide him to whatever extent is necessary to have him complete the act.

91. Q. Should I spank him after an accident?
   A. No.

92. Q. After an accident, should I get dry pants and change his pants for him?
   A. No: have him do it himself, with manual guidance from you.

93. Q. Suppose my child wets his pants right at the start of training?
   A. Then give only the verbal disapproval and have him change himself.

94. Q. What do I do if my child gets stubborn and has a tantrum or refuses to follow my instructions?
   A. Do not argue. Calmly repeat your instruction, gently but firmly guide him through the instructed action, and praise him the instant he starts to follow your instruction.

95. Q. If my child is not trained at the end of the day, should I put diapers back on him and start all over the next day?
   A. No. Dress him in underpants and the next morning start where you left off.

97. Q. During the first week after training, what do I do about a) accidents; b) wearing diapers at night; c) giving snack treats and approval for his pottying; d) giving approval for his dry pants; e) his outer clothing?
   A. Show your disapproval, have him practice

toileting, and have him change his pants; b) Except for very young children, discontinue diapers at night; c) Discontinue the snack treats and approval for pottying; d) Schedule at least six pants inspections each day, with praise given for dry pants; e) Dress him only in loose outer clothing that you have taught him to manage himself.

98. Q. How should I treat a bowel accident?

A. The same as a wetting accident.

99. Q. After a week without accidents, how should I react to an isolated accident?

A. Show disapproval and require him to change his wet pants.

REMINDER LIST OF TRAINING MATERIALS AND SUPPLIES*

Potty Chair: The type that is easily emptied. See page 52.

Doll That Wets. See page 54.

Training Pants: About eight pairs with very loosely fitting waist and leg openings. See pages 56-57.

Drinks: Such as soda, punch, water. See page 51.

Snack Treats: Potato chips, peanuts, corn chips, fruit slices, candy. See page 50.

Reminder Lists. See Chapter 7, page 159.

Friends-Who-Care List. See page 55.

Sponge or Cleaning Cloth. See page 103.

Toilet Tissue or Facial Tissue. See page 121.

Apron or dress with a pocket for carrying snack treats. See page 51.

* The page numbers refer to where detailed descriptions are given for each item.

PROMPTING AND INSPECTION REMINDERS

Time of Pants Inspections

(To be given every five minutes until pottying is self-initiated; then about every fifteen minutes.)

In the Blanks, Write in the Time of Each Pants Inspection to Serve as a Reminder as to When You Should Conduct the Next Inspection.

1	2	3	4	5	6	7	8
9	10	11	12	13	14	15	16
17	18	19	20	21	22	23	24
25	26	27	28	29	30	31	32
33	34	35	36	37	38	39	40
41	42	43	44	45	46	47	48
49	50	51	52	53	54	55	56
57	58	59	60	61	62	63	64
65	66	67	68	69	70	71	72
73	74	75					

Time of Prompted Toiletings
(Child should toilet about every fifteen minutes until pottying is self-initiated; then discontinue.)

TOILET TRAINING IN LESS THAN A DAY

In the Blanks, Write in the Time of Each Prompted Toileting to Serve as a Reminder as to When You Should Start the Next Prompted Toileting.

1	2	3	4	5	6	7	8
9	10	11	12	13	14	15	16
17	18	19	20	21	22	23	24
25							

In the Blanks, Write in the Time of Each Accident.

1	2	3	4	5	

174

REMINDER SHEET: AFTER-TRAINING PANTS INSPECTIONS

(Simply check off each empty space when you conduct the pants inspection.)

DAYS AFTER TRAINING

	1st	2nd	3rd	4th	5th	6th	7th	8th	9th	10th
Before Breakfast										
Before Midmorning Snack Period										
Before Lunch										
Before Afternoon Snack Period										
Before Nap										
Before Dinner										
Before Bedtime										
Other ————										
Other ————										

Mental Retardation

This section describes the types of changes in the training procedure that are needed when the child suffers from mild or moderate mental retardation. If your child has normal intelligence, you need not read this section.

Why Normal Intelligence Speeds Up the New Training Procedure

The new method relies heavily on the ability of the child to understand language and to use his imagination. The Friends-Who-Care procedure assumes that the child is able to imagine what his friends will say. The Doll-That-Wets procedure assumes that the child is able to identify with, and to imitate, the actions of the doll. The Verbal Rehearsal procedure assumes that the child can understand simple instructions. To the extent that a child has a normal ability to understand language, to use his imagination, and to imitate, that child will be able to understand more quickly what he is supposed to do and why he should do it. Otherwise, the learning must depend more on repeated associations, repeated practice, gestures, and manual guidance and will require more time.

At What Age Should the Retarded Child Be Trained?

The retarded child should be given more time to develop physically, socially and mentally before you initiate the training. The greater the retardation, the longer you should wait. In general, toilet training should not be started until 30 months of age if your child is obviously retarded. If the retardation is severe, even more time may be needed for development. By five years of age, even severely retarded children (I.Q. about 30) may be trained.

Change in the Doll-That-Wets Procedure for Retarded Children

Learning by imitation and learning by teaching are achieved by the Doll-That-Wets procedure. Yet retarded children are often unable to identify with a doll. You should attempt to use the doll in training your retarded child just as you would with a normally developed child. If, however, the child pays no attention to the doll, throws the doll away, or is unable to understand the meaning of the doll's actions, you should discontinue the use of the doll entirely. For children whose I.Q. is below 20, the doll will probably have no meaning and you will not be able to use it. If the child has played with dolls in the past, you probably will be able to use the Doll-That-Wets procedure.

Use of the Friends-Who-Care Procedure with Retarded Children

The use of the Friends-Who-Care procedure assumes that the child has several friends other than his mother, that he can identify them by name, and that he cares what they think of him. The retarded child may not have learned to do these things, especially if the child is in an institution where he has not formed close attachments to specific adults. A measure of the child's ability in this respect is to tell him to point to (or to approach) a specifically named person when other persons are also present and observe whether he goes to that specifically named person. If he is unable to do so, do not attempt to use the Friends-Who-Care procedure. Instead, rely entirely on your own approval.

Other Changes in Procedure for the Retarded Child

In addition to the changes noted above, many other changes in procedure are needed for the retarded individual. The instructor should use manual guidance extensively. He must use gestures whenever he speaks. His instructions must be very simple. Longer periods of sitting on the potty or toilet seat are required. If the retarded person is in an institution, special procedures are needed to ensure that the institutional staff members will be able to conduct the instruction. These procedures are described in great detail in a previous book by the authors that deals specifically with the problem of toilet-training retarded individuals, especially those who are institutionalized (see Foxx and Azrin, *Toilet Training the Retarded* in the Reference Section).

References

Azrin, N. H. and Foxx, R. M. "A Rapid Method of Toilet Training the Institutionalized Retarded." *Journal of Applied Behavior Analysis,* 1971, 4, 88–99.

Azrin, N. H., Sneed, T. J. and Foxx, R. M. "Dry Bed: A Rapid Method of Eliminating Bedwetting (Enuresis) of the Retarded." *Behaviour Research and Therapy,* 1973.

Foxx, R. M. and Azrin, N. H. "Dry Pants: A Rapid Method of Toilet Training Children." *Behaviour Research and Therapy,* 1973a.

Foxx, R. M. and Azrin, N. H. *Toilet Training the Retarded: A Rapid Program for Day and Nighttime Independent Toileting.* Champaign, Illinois, Research Press Company, 1973b.

INDEX

INDEX

185

Nathan H. Azrin, Ph.D., is the father of four children and a leading authority on the psychology of learning. He currently heads the Behavior Research Laboratory at Anna State Hospital, Anna, Illinois, and is Professor of Rehabilitation at Southern Illinois University.

A *cum laude* graduate of Boston University, Dr. Azrin received his Ph.D. in psychology in 1956 at Harvard University, where he helped develop programmed arithmetic instruction for primary-school children. He was a research associate at the Boston University School of Medicine and also participated in experimental studies of learning disabilities in children. Before taking his present post in Illinois in 1957, he was a research psychologist at the Institute of Living in Hartford, Connecticut, and performed studies of learning and motivation factors while serving in the United States Army.

Dr. Azrin has been a lecturer in the Psychology Department of Harvard University. He is a member and fellow of the American Psychological Association, and a past president of both the Society of the Experimental Analysis of Behavior and Division 25 of the American Psychological Association. He has been an editor of the *Journal of Applied Behavior*

Analysis and the *Journal of the Experimental Analysis of Behavior*.

Dr. Azrin has published over 100 studies in the field of learning and psychological treatment. He is co-author (with Teodoro Ayllon) of *The Token Economy: A Motivational System for Therapy and Rehabilitation* and (with Richard M. Foxx) of *Toilet Training the Retarded*.

Richard M. Foxx, Ph.D., is a research psychologist for the state of Illinois Department of Mental Health, affiliated with the Behavior Research Laboratory, Anna State Hospital, Anna, Illinois, where he develops intensive learning programs for the institutionalized mentally ill and retarded and training programs for out-patient children both normal and retarded.

A graduate of the University of California (Riverside) and California State University (Fullerton), Dr. Foxx received his Ph.D. in educational psychology from Southern Illinois University in 1971 with a dissertation on the use of overcorrection procedures in a classroom for retarded children. As a Research Assistant at Patton State Hospital, Patton, California, and at Pacific State Hospital, Pomona, California, he worked in remotivation programs for the adult mentally ill and for retarded adolescent females.

Dr. Foxx currently teaches a course in child psychology at Southern Illinois University. He is a member of the American Psychological Association and of the Child Psychology, Experimental Analysis of Behavior, Clinical Psychology and Mental Retardation divisions within that association. He is also a member of the National Society for Autistic

Children, the Association for the Advancement of Behavior Therapy and the American Association on Mental Deficiency.

Dr. Foxx has published widely on the learning process and developed many educational programs for both normal and disordered individuals. He is co-author (with Nathan H. Azrin) of *Toilet Training the Retarded*.

Bringing Up A Brighter, Happier Child

The growth of a child's mind is a wonderful thing to watch. And it's even more wonderful when you've read up on the subject. Pocket Books has a fine list of titles about the mental development of children written by prominent specialists in the field.

If you are a parent, or soon plan to be, you'll want these books for your home library.

_____	50897	HOW TO RAISE A BRIGHTER CHILD Joan Beck	$3 95
_____	55442	IMPROVING YOUR CHILD'S BEHAVIOR CHEMISTRY Lendon Smith, MD	$3.95
_____	55445	UNDERSTANDING YOUR CHILD FROM BIRTH TO THREE Joseph Church	$3.50
_____	55444	TEACH YOUR BABY MATH Glenn Doman	$2.95